Just Ask

Just Ask

A Survival Guide for Today's Economy

Chris Hetherman

Contents

Introduction

I want to start off my book with a short overview of how I came up with the idea of writing a book based on "Just Asking" principles. In each chapter, you will learn not only about asking others for help but also some of the questions you should be asking your internal self to help you financially. The purpose of this book is not to make everyone a millionaire—even though if you use the principles I outline in each chapter, you will have the opportunity to become wealthier than you could imagine. My book was written to help you so that you may be able to help others. Helping others is about more than giving people money. The best thing you can do is help them figure out why they are in the situation they are in. Sometimes it is lack of discipline, and sometimes it is bad luck. However, listening to a person and showing them you care can be a great help. I hope you will keep that in mind as you read on. I look forward to your feedback on my website: JustAskTheBook.com.

When my wife and I graduated college and were first married, we moved out West to Washington State to acquire internships. Before we even got to Washington State, we were already using some of my "Just Ask" principles and did not even know it. The jobs we put in for were closed to applications, but we were able to contact the hiring department directly and get our applications in for the jobs we ended up being hired for by just asking them to please accept our late applications.

When we moved out West, we had very little money and could not afford to stay at a hotel. It was just my wife, our English Springer Spaniel, and me crammed in a regular cab compact pickup truck (Chevy S-10) with all our belongings stuffed in every crack and crevice in the back of the truck with the topper on it. The truck was packed so tightly we had underwear and socks stuffed in any available space in the back of the truck. We kept hoping the topper would not pop off or it would look like a confetti popper with our things flying all over. Since we were new to the area and afraid of approaching people to inquire about where to find a place to stay, we drove around and finally found a place that looked approachable.

It was a modest-sized house with great landscaping in a nice-looking neighborhood that appeared to be safe. There were several nice cars in the driveway and on the street. We stopped and knocked on the door and some people came to the door and we shared that we were from out of state, had jobs in the area, and were looking for a place to stay/rent. We just asked them if they were able to provide us any help. The people who came to the door were very nice to us and gave us guidance to go and see the pastor at the local church for help. We thought about taking their advice, but our pride got in the way and we did not go to the church. If only we would have just asked, who knows how our lives might have been different. Instead, we ended up sleeping in our truck overnight on top of a Power Plant Dam where we were soon to be working.

The funny thing is, about a year later, we started going to a church in the same town where we met the same people who owned the home we stopped at when we first arrived. They always felt bad that they sent us away and wished they would have put us up for the night. We always laugh together about that time. The rest is history, and we are still great friends today. I dedicate part of this book to Laura, who died after a seven-year battle with cancer, and we are thankful for the blessed times we had with her over the last twenty years. She was always such a giving person and would always "Just Ask" others how she could help them, long before they would ever ask for help.

I grew up in a home that had a lot of physical issues. Whenever it would rain the house would flood and the walls would get wet, and we experienced damp musty, mildew smells. The bottom of the low-quality wood dressers splintered from getting wet, the wood swelled and expanded, and the boards started to fall apart beneath. There was a weird, pungent odor about the home that was not very pleasing, but it was still associated with home. However, I did not know anything different at the time so it was normal to me. The house seemed to be barely insulated, and it was always drafty around the windows and doors. The tile floors were falling apart and were always cold and wet, so we wore shoes and boots in the house. The single pane windows would sometimes fall out from the glazing drying out and rotting away. When I got a little bit older, I remember trying to help replace the windows to be able to keep the draft out, but I was not very good at glazing windows. I put plastic over the outside by pounding little strips of wood around there to prevent the wind from coming through. The front door of the house was a big, white, solid wood door, but it wouldn't open because we had to jam newspaper around it to prevent wind from coming through. The bottom was stuffed with newspaper as well. Whenever it would flood, we pulled out the old, wet newspaper from around the bottom of the door and replaced it.

On cold mornings I sat in my bedroom on top of the heater by my window to keep warm. To get to my room from other areas of the house I had to walk down the dirt floor hallway. We, as children, slept in a drafty garage that was converted into two bedrooms: a boys' room and a girls' room. My bedroom floor was some type of splintery plywood with nails that would sometimes pop up and tear into my feet as I walked by. When I was fourteen, my neighbor threw their old carpet in the trash. I took it and placed it on the floor in my room and was super happy to be able to have carpet. This was the first time I had something soft under my feet, and it felt so good and made my room more homey. In fact, my friend, whose parents threw out the carpet, helped me install it. The light in my bedroom was a "temporary" two-wire light bulb hanging from the ceiling with two wire nuts, which ended up being permanent for all the years I lived there. This was usually the first thing to break when my brother and I were horsing around or throwing things at each other.

The room was only partially paneled, and there was an open door frame into the bedroom so anyone could look in. The ceiling was roughed-in drywall in my room, and my sisters' room had a similar setup, except there was a large hole in the ceiling drywall where my father fell through when he was working on the old oil furnace up in the attic. My oldest sister remembers when my father fell through the attic. She told me how bad she felt to see my dad dangling there with broken ribs and a broken arm and there was nothing she could do to help. She had to get my dad's friend to help get him out. I'm glad I didn't have to see that, but the hole always reminded me of the event.

I remember when the electricity was off and having to cook hotdogs over the gas heater in my room. I remember the house being very hot in the summer and extremely cold in the winter. In the summer, I would open up my windows, which had no screens, needing to let some air in. The mosquitoes would come in as well and would bite us all night long. The mosquitoes always seemed to like to bite me more than anyone else in the family. It was a little scary sometimes laying there with the window open and just a sheet draped over the window in place of curtains. There were many nights I dreamed of someone sneaking in the house or thought I heard sounds outside the window and would get scared and run to the other side of the home.

Our house did get broken into many times over the years. Our bikes would constantly get stolen whenever we forgot to bring them into the house. Every time we would save up money and purchase something, someone would come by and steal it. I would think at some point whoever was stealing our stuff would have felt bad and stopped, but it just continued. We really didn't live in a bad neighborhood from what I recall. We had an acre of land and lived directly behind a Kmart, so maybe it was just that people would come from the Kmart parking lot and steal.

There were a couple of events, though, that haunted me for a while. Once on the night before Halloween, someone took a slingshot and launched a two-inch steel nut through our window. It went right over my bed where I was sleeping and smashed into the wall. I remember being so tired that I actually fell back asleep and was asleep when the police came to investigate. We never did find out who broke our window, but it took a long time before we were able to replace that window. I taped plastic over it for a long period of time. Another time the neighbor who lived next door had a big party with a band playing and a lot of drinking. When the band stopped playing for the night, someone broke a window over our bed while I was sleeping. The glass shattered over my bed and fell all over my head. Fortunately, I was not hurt. I was thankful this happened during the summer. If it would have happened in the winter, my room would have been even colder than it always was.

Shooting Mice in the Wall

My son likes the story I tell him about when I was sick and had to stay home from school and how I took an old Red Ryder BB gun and shot mice when they came out of the holes in the wall. I know this is not humane to some people, but we could not keep the mice out due to the poor construction of the home. I would have rather kept the cute little creatures outside where they could flourish. I know my sisters and brother would not have considered us poor at the time, but I can tell you that we all learned early that we had to work to survive.

Blessed to Experience a Time When We Lacked Money

After college, my wife and I moved out West and experienced a time where we were flat broke. We had been working a seasonal government job, and at the end of the season, we traveled back to the Midwest to visit family. We were set to collect unemployment until our job started back up in early spring. However, the checks were mailed to the wrong address, and we ended up with no checks, and the government would not issue any new checks for six months.

Fortunately; while working we met a person who asked us if we needed any help. He and his wife were the kind of people who enjoyed helping others, and my wife and I were the type of people who would never think to "Just Ask" for help at that time. By asking our friend if he knew of any places for rent, we found a place in a small town of two hundred people, thanks to his help. He told the landlord we were trustworthy, and he convinced them we would be good renters and would pay rent as soon as we were back to work. All he did was ask the landlord to trust us for the rent until our jobs started, and it worked out well for all parties involved.

I remember moving into the double-wide home he had found for us. We were just out of college and had no money, except a credit card. Our ramen noodles and other dry goods went missing due to the mice that inhabited the house. Looking back, I should have asked the landlord to help remedy the situation, but at that time we were at the beginning of learning the "Just Ask" principles. Thankfully, our good friends visited us and were kind enough to leave us a frozen pizza and a case of soda to get us by for a while.

When I turned the oven on, I smelled the most awful, pungent, ammonia-like smell I had ever smelled. My friend knew right away the smell was that of mice urine. It was a putrid smell, but there was not much I could do, being that we had no money. We ended up taking the stove apart together and replacing the insulation, which was laden with mouse urine, droppings, and dead rotten mice. I did not know enough to tell the landlord that he should provide us with a working stove, and my friend was too nice to ask.

Our friends encouraged us to go into town and ask for food from the local food bank. I can still remember actually crying as we went in to "Just Ask" for some help with food. There was a gut-wrenching feeling of having to go to the local food bank and collect a bag of the food in black and white containers, which stated something like "for Government subsidy". All I really remember in the bag was cornbread mix, peanut butter, and some type of cheese block. Even though I grew up poor, this hit me really hard. I felt like we were begging and that I could not provide for ourselves. Growing up it always seemed like we could earn enough money to get by, and having to go to others for help was not in my nature. Looking back, this was one of the best experiences that helped build me into the person I am today. It allowed us to appreciate all that we had, even if it was very little, and want to help others.

Even though I want to help others, people sometimes like to take a statement and make it negative when it is meant for good. The information I have written in my book is based on my own experiences and is as accurate and clear as I can remember. I am in no way claiming to be an expert in finances or any of the topics I cover, and you have to do what is right for you and your finances. I cannot guarantee you will have the same success I have using my techniques to save money, but in my opinion, my principles can work for about anyone with bills to pay. It does not matter if you are poor or rich. Think of the "Just Ask" principle as a workout routine; the more you exercise the principles, the better and more efficient you'll get at making them work for you. Some of the characters mentioned in the following chapters are fictional and used as examples only to help you understand a principle. My own experiences are told to the best of my recollection and are in no way intended to do anything except help you understand my thought process. I hope you will be able to save enough money with my techniques and principles listed in my book that you will buy your friend a book, and your friend will buy their friend a book, and so on.

It has been a challenge to write this book, but every so often I get inspired again by other people or events that call me back to writing to help people. Over the course of writing this book, I was able to become motivated by a few people. However, the number one person I can thank is a friend by the name of Richard. He wrote a book that speaks of the philosophy of us having a higher purpose in life, which I myself believe in. I just need to change my life to allow the time I do have to focus on more important things, like helping people, rather than working to achieve more material possessions. Don't get me wrong; I don't drive an exotic car or live in a large, fancy house, but we are blessed to have all we need and to be able to help others. In fact, I am dedicating at least 10% of the profits from this book to a charitable trust for helping others.

The next source of inspiration came from Kevin Trudeau's books. My friend shared some books on finance with me authored by Kevin Trudeau. I read his books and could not see how they would truly be helpful to anyone except the author by filling his pockets with more money. It seemed as if he was selling some great secrets someone did not want us to know about. It reminded me of a story I had heard as a child when a person sold a book on TV about his secret to becoming a millionaire. The book basically stated that selling the book, which in my parents' opinion contained no useful information, made the author a millionaire. I am not sure if the story is true or if it's a story my parents made up.

However, I was not surprised when millionaire and bestselling author Kevin Trudeau was arrested for making false claims in his books. How can a book make people an instant millionaire and help them gain so much so quickly? I believe the old adage, "If it sounds too good to be true, it probably is." In Kevin Trudeau's case, it ended up being more about money than helping people. His situation drove me forward in writing again because there are many people who could use my help. Saving a little money to some people is a lot, and to those who have a lot of money, saving more money allows them to be able to share more and help others. My desire is for everyone who purchases my book to share it and its principles with others. I don't expect everyone to buy my book, but if it helps them, I hope they will pass it on or encourage others who can afford to purchase it. I believe anyone who buys my book will save more than they pay for it, but if someone can't afford it, please share your book with them if you are fortunate enough to own one.

As I sit here and write the chapters to my book, I cannot help but think that if a person is to take anything away from reading my book, it is simply "**Just Ask**™©". What I mean by "Just Ask" will become evident as you read my chapters.

Chapter 1
Time Is Money

In this chapter you will learn the value of understanding the relationship between time and money. Money is an unlimited resource, and your time is limited. By understanding your own core values, you will be able to make choices in your life that help you not only financially but also physically and emotionally. Also, in this chapter you will learn how cutting costs can cost you, how to use your skills to save money, when quality is important, how to know your limitations, and how to determine the example you are setting to others.

Cutting Costs Can Cost You
One of the things you need to do is "Just Ask" yourself if cutting costs will save you time and money. Many times we try to save a few pennies and it ends up costing us several dollars. For example, if you buy a cheap tool to use on a project and it breaks and ruins what you were working on or you have to go back to the store several times to exchange it, was the tool really worth the upfront savings? Most likely not. After all your time and money is spent, you might realize you actually lost money by having to drive back and forth to correct the issue; maybe you had to redo your work because the tool didn't do it right the first time and you lost some of your valuable time. I have been guilty of doing this in the past and have now trained myself to ask the right questions. As you read my book, I will give guidance so you can train yourself in things that will not only save you money but also provide you more time and money to enjoy things that bring you value while helping others.

My Father Dies Unexpectedly and My World Changes
When I was thirteen years old, my father passed away unexpectedly and my family's life turned upside down. I had many changes in my life at that point, including changing grade schools in the middle of the year. It seemed as if time had stopped for a while. I came to the realization that time is precious and limited and you never know when your last day will be. This realization might have been a curse to some, but for me it was a blessing because I was given the insight that you only get one chance to live. My philosophy that you cannot take your time for granted helped me

find value in helping people who cannot help themselves, especially when it comes to older people who have so much experience, wisdom, and value in what they have to offer.

After my father died, I started working for a small construction company at three dollars an hour. I worked after school and on the weekend for a neighbor who was an old-school Italian and worked very hard and was very frugal. I worked for his company until I went to college, and even then I tended to help him out during the summer when I was off from school. I always appreciated my neighbor giving me that job, even though I had to work very hard for little money. I did a lot of the grunt work, such as tearing things out, breaking cement, and scraping walls down to prepare for painting. The nice thing was the person I worked for took the time to explain why he did things as we were working. I learned a few things from my neighbor. I learned to work hard. I learned that if one is patient, there is a lot you can do with a little material. I also learned there was a trade-off between time and money. It always seemed like if I had money, I had no time, and vice versa.

Time Is Limited While Money Is Unlimited

Theoretically, there is an unlimited amount of money out there for you to make, yet you have a limited amount of time to live. When you're choosing what to spend your time and money on, it's important to consider the value of both. It is very uncommon for people to have a large amount of time and money. So, whenever you're making a decision about where to focus your time and money, you need to "Just Ask" yourself if the time you're spending is worth the money you're saving, or if the money you're spending is worth the time you're saving.

If you buy a cheap, slow computer that doesn't meet your family needs, ask yourself what value it brings. By purchasing a slow computer, will you need to stay later at the office and away from your family to get more work done? Does it mean your child will have to stay later at school or go to a library to accomplish a task because the home computer is too slow? Will the slow computer use up time your child could have been at home learning more and spending time with the family? Will it end up costing you more money because now you need to spend gas taking your child to the library to get work done? Will you be spending more time and money on refreshments and food while you are out of the house? Do you sacrifice eating healthy to save time?

All these are good questions to ask when you are looking at the time and money relationship. You can evaluate the time and money relationship with almost everything you do. However, most of the time, this is a subconscious decision you make that you don't think about much.

When Quality Counts

When you try to save money, you have to be aware that quality can be an important part of your decision. For example, if you knew you needed to have open-heart surgery, would you put in a cheap heart valve or the best you could afford? I'm sure you would have them put in a heart valve that is known to be quality and will last as long as possible. As I'll share with you in greater detail later on in this book, there are certain things that might cost more money in the long run if you don't go for adequate quality from the start. You may spend more money replacing or repairing an item. It's important that you continue to ask yourself what you need and what quality level will meet your needs for the duration of the time you need it.

Use Your Skills to Save Time and Money

We all have different gifts and talents, and sometimes these can be hidden, and you might even forget you have them. "Just Ask" yourself what your talents might be and what you enjoy doing as part of your self-reflection. Sometimes the talents you have can bring you joy, relaxation, exercise, and other benefits as well as save you money.

For example, if cooking brings you enjoyment, you could do that for your family or yourself and save yourself money instead of going out to restaurants. You could make healthy food, which in turn might extend your lifespan and provide you more time to do the things you enjoy. You should ask yourself if there are things you enjoy doing that you may be paying other people to do for you. For example, if you like to work on vehicles, consider changing the oil and brakes on your vehicles yourself, which would save you money. If you like to do your own gardening, landscaping, or home repairs, you can save money and gain a sense of accomplishment.

Doing some of the work yourself would be a great example for your family and others. Not only can you save some money, but you might be able to involve others and teach them as well. Every person's preference of what they find joy in is different. However, there is always something you can turn into a healthy, relaxing, cost-saving hobby you enjoy and possibly share with others. It can bring a person much joy and satisfaction to do their own work as well as save money.

However, you still have to ask yourself if you have the time, talent, and skills to meet your needs. If you don't have the talent and skills, then you need to ask yourself if there is a way to learn them and if you would enjoy learning something new. I use YouTube to learn how to do mechanical things sometimes. I am sure there are many other services, websites, and forums that can help you. Visit JustAskTheBook.com for a list of links to help you.

Stop Rationalizing Poor Choices
Ask yourself, will doing something to save money have a negative impact on your career or life? Not going to the doctor because it will cost money, eating poorly rather than taking the time to learn how to cook, or not exercising because you can't afford to go to the gym can all have a negative impact on your life. I know as humans we can rationalize anything to justify why we make the choices we do. However, you have to "Just Ask" if your decisions are the best ones for you overall. If you focus on saving money so much that you make poor spending decisions, you will end up paying more in the future to correct your poor decisions.

For example, when I say eating poorly rather than learning to cook might have a negative impact on your life, what I am saying is that you could end up with medical issues that take up a lot more of your money and time than if you had spent a little more time and money to eat healthful foods. If you work your whole life to make money and spend a lot of time accumulating wealth so you have a lot of money when you retire, how good will it be if you end up not being able to do the things you enjoy? Instead, you could be spending your last days spending all the money you worked so hard to save on doctors and hospitals. People often work extra hours today only to spend their money tomorrow trying to get back some of the health they lost. I know too many people who are living for tomorrow instead of today and plan as if they will have the same health in retirement to do all the things they did not have time for when they were younger.

Everything You Own, Owns a Piece of You
Remember that you only have so much time, so you always have to think about the trade-off between time and money. When you look at your time, consider whether hiring a person to do a job

would save time and if doing the job yourself would be worth the money saved. Most people don't have a lot of time and a lot of money. Generally, people with a lot of money spend their time trying to figure out how to protect and keep their money and make it grow. Even though they could use their money to free up time, they often don't.

It is in our nature to want more and more, and sometimes we don't know when to stop and be satisfied with what we have. On the other hand, people with a lot of time are generally spending all their time trying to get more money. If we could be satisfied with a simple life, we would likely be compelled to give more and help other people out. This comes down to asking yourself when enough is enough. A good way to figure this out is to write down all your needs and goals so that when you achieve them, you can be satisfied. Be cautious as you accumulate more wealth because you will find that everything you own, owns a piece of you. That means all your possessions will be taking up your time. For example, when you get a large home, you have to spend more money on furniture, taxes, utilities, cleaning, painting, landscaping, and so on.

Ask yourself what you really need to be satisfied. If you figure it out before you get there, you are more likely to be satisfied when you arrive. However, if you have no goals, you could be searching forever only to be continually disappointed.

What Example Are You Setting?

When analyzing the value of your time versus your money, ask yourself what type of example you want to set for others. Will your children see value in saving money and the satisfaction you get from doing things yourself? Will there be something gained by your teaching your family how to do something and be independent? Are you teaching good environmental resource conservation by repairing something rather than replacing it?

I love to work on mechanical things, so I find joy in working on our vehicles. I try to share the love of this with my children by providing an opportunity for them to learn how to do basic repairs on vehicles. When sharing with them, they get a sense of the work and tools required to do the repair along with what it would have cost if we took it to a repair shop. When I tell them we just spent two hours saving $400, their eyes light up like they just won a small lottery. Vehicle repairs can be costly. Most technicians charge rates of $80 per hour. So if you only are earning less than that, you have a monetary incentive to do the repairs yourself.

However, not everyone is mechanically inclined or enjoys working on these types of things. I am sure if you "Just Ask" yourself, you'll come up with something you enjoy doing that saves money and teaches value. Keep in mind that you always have a decision to make, and you have to ask the question, what will happen if I don't fix it? My friend's parents had a small plastic piece break off inside their dryer, and they chose not to replace the part. The dryer still worked and dried clothes, but it began tearing holes in their clothes. So, saving time and money by not fixing the dryer ended up costing them money in new clothes, and they still had to fix the dryer anyway. This goes hand in hand with the old adage, "penny-wise and pound-foolish."

Two things I ask when considering a project are: (1) what value will it have? and (2) how will it impact others? Another question to ask is, how will your actions allow you to help others? For example, will the extra money you save enable you to give more to your church, or will it give you more time to give back in a charitable manner? If you don't have extra money, can you help others by using your skills in a charitable manner? I have spent time with people helping them figure out how to get out of credit card debt and pay their bills, which you will learn more about in the upcoming chapters.

Beyond "Just Ask"

The purpose of spending my valuable and limited time writing this book is to help others train themselves to "Just Ask" themselves the right questions and to value the decisions they're making regarding time and money. I also want to encourage you to "Just Ask" others for help. You will see more examples of "Just Asking" as you continue to read on, but keep in mind that "Just Ask" goes beyond asking for a discount on a purchase at a store. It is asking you to look deeper and reflect on your values and what you want other people to see and learn by your actions.

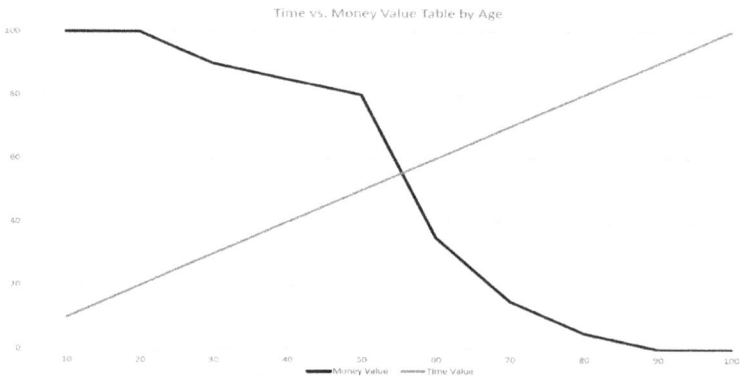

Time vs. Money Value Table by Age

"Just Ask" Yourself

- How much time do you really have?
- What is the value of doing something yourself, and do you have or can you learn the skills?
- How much money do you really need to be content?
- Is money or time more valuable to you at this point in your life?

"Just Ask" Others

- Ask for help from others who have done it.
- Ask others what is the best tool for the job.
- Ask retailers or service providers if you can get a discount.
- Ask for discounts if you offer to buy a higher quality item, which is more expensive.

"Just Ask" Savings

"I asked for a discount on a new door, which was on clearance, and I saved $670."

—Dean D., Stevens Point, WI

"I asked DEWALT for a replacement battery for my tools because it quit charging. It was almost three years old, and by just spending two minutes on a call, they replaced two older batteries with brand new ones, which saved me over $100."

—Chris S., Roseville, MI

"I asked a company that repaired cars if they sold paint for a car part and explained that it was a gift and wanted their opinion on how to fix it. They offered to do the whole part and only charged me $25 for the paint. It would have taken me several hours to do what they did for free. I just had to be patient, and when they were painting a car the same color, they painted my part. It only took them a few days to do this, and it saved me time."

—Terry C., Pasco, WA

"I asked a restaurant for free french fries when I had to wait a long time for my order, and they gave me a free order of fries and a drink. This happens all the time to me just by asking with a smile on my face and not being rude. I am asking for a favor, and they don't owe me free things. They have given me free shakes, fries, cookies, even meals by being friendly."

—Lisa H.

"I asked the phone company to reduce their bill for the same service, and it saved several hundred dollars annually."

—Connie S., Plover, WI

"I bought a brand new STIHL tool, and it was already on sale, but by asking, the owner gave me some oil and an additional $30 discount."

—Mark R., Stevens Point, WI

"I had a friend whose $30 shirt had a pocket that had unstitched and they were about to throw it out. I stitched it up in two minutes and the shirt was as good as new. I received a soda for the help, and it saved him $30 on a new shirt."

—Tonya V., Wisconsin Rapids, WI

Chapter 2
Paying Bills

In this chapter you will learn techniques you can use to save money on paying bills by just asking the important questions to your providers. Also, you will learn to evaluate what your bills are and to ask yourself if you truly need all the things you have that are costing you money and contributing to your bills. I will be sharing some of the things I have done to reduce the cost of bills and make them easier to pay, along with some additional techniques for saving money.

In my late teens, it was difficult for me to remember to pay my bills on time. I would get charged a late fee, and they would send an even larger bill the next month and increase my interest rate for being late. This would cause me to spend a lot of my precious time calling the company trying to get the charges reversed. Sometimes I was successful in convincing customer service representatives to remove the late charge and reverse the interest increase when a bill was late by just asking. Sometimes I was not successful in having the charges reversed. What I learned was that I was not responsible enough to manage my accounts nor did I understand the importance of managing my accounts so that I didn't put myself in debt.

Even though you may not always be successful, I recommend that you call—whether it be a credit card company, utility company, or any other company that sends you a bill—and "Just Ask" if they are willing to reduce or remove your late fees or interest charges. The worst thing that could happen is the company says no. If you have not asked for any favors from them in the past and you have a record of paying your bills on time, they are more likely to help you out. Sometimes the first person you speak to may not be able to approve the changes to your account in which case you should ask to speak with a supervisor. The key thing is to be polite and respectful to the people you speak with and "Just Ask." I believe in the old adage that you get more flies with honey than vinegar, so be extra nice and you may get a little forgiveness if you ever need it. Also, I have found the longer you are willing to be calm, patient, and continue to keep finding things to speak with the representative about, the more successful you will be. I have not figured out if this is because they get worn out from speaking or if they genuinely want to help me out. Maybe it is a combination of both.

Set up Automatic Payments and Don't Get Charged Late Fees Again

To avoid late payments, you can set up automatic payments for most accounts. For example, on my automobile and home insurance, I make sure that payments are automatic out of my checking account. Also, things like my AAA membership are set up to charge my credit card automatically, then my credit card is set up to be paid automatically from my bank account. It is sort of like a payment domino effect, except I keep myself from getting late fees. Be sure you have enough money in your checking account so that you don't overdraw on your account and incur penalties there.

With things like automobile insurance, I determine if they charge an added fee if I don't pay the six-month balance in full. If that is not the case, I set up automatic payments to come out of my checking account each month so that I can keep the money in my money market account collecting interest until the next minimum payment is due. By doing this, I am able to keep more cash freed up and collecting interest instead of making one big payment to cover my six-month premium. Most of the time I found that if I pay only the monthly amount for an insurance bill, they charge me about five dollars extra per month, which adds up to $60 for the year. I will not set up an automatic payment if they have a fee associated with it. Some accounts may give you a discount if you pay your bill in full. If that is the case, I pay the bill in full if I can afford it. Also, some companies will give you a price break if you set up automatic payments out of your checking account.

Some people worry about giving out their bank account number and information. You should ask your bank about the risk associated with setting up automatic payments and make sure that you're not responsible if someone or some company over-draws your account without proper approval. My bank account will not be charged a fee for any unscrupulous transaction I have not authorized.

Please keep in mind if you "Just Ask," a company representative can walk you through the process of setting up an automatic payment. Often you can select the day of the month on which to draw the payment. Sometimes it is as easy as going online and filling in your bank information. For safety precautions, the company will usually send you a small amount of money to your bank account to confirm the right information is set up for routing. They will then ask you to confirm the amount that was transferred to your bank account in order to finalize the automatic payment. This assures that they and you are not sending information to other people. You can always change the way your automatic payment works or cancel it completely if you like.

Medical Bill Payments Made Easy, or as Easy as Possible
Medical payments can sometimes be reduced if you call the provider and share with them what your insurance did not cover and ask them if you can get some type of discount. Also, you can tell your provider if you don't have insurance, and they might provide you a lower rate than people with insurance. The reason they do this is because sometimes an insurance company will pay only a portion of a set treatment, and they charge more to assure that they get as close to their needed cost as possible. The healthcare provider might then choose to absorb the rest of the cost instead of passing it on to the consumer after the insurance has paid their amount.

Don't ignore a medical bill, even if you cannot afford to pay the bill at this time. The medical provider would always rather work with a patient than send them to a collection agency, and most patients would rather work with the medical provider than be sent to a collection agency. Collection agencies are paid to hound you until they get your money, and the medical provider pays them a typical fee of about thirty cents on every dollar they recover. I have experience with this personally when I was trying to set up my health savings account for a new company I was working for. I was taking money out of my paycheck every month to put into the account; however, the company did not transfer the money into the account, and my health savings account was tied up in their system. I had medical bills due, so I called the healthcare provider and explained my situation to them. They were willing to work with me and told me to call him back within a month so that I would not get sent to collections. I called back several months in a row as I tried to get the money freed up.

I got so busy one month I missed one of the deadlines to contact the healthcare provider, and they sent me to a collection agency. It didn't affect my credit, but it became a real nuisance because they demanded their money in full up-front and wouldn't wait for my account to be finalized. Fortunately, I was able to get the account finalized before the due date, but I had to pay everything in full. The healthcare provider was willing to work with me to set up a payment plan, even if it was just a few dollars a month, to assure I was paying him back. I chose to be stubborn and not pay anything until my health savings account was active. I then paid the price because my phone would continually ring with automated messages from the collection agency. I wanted to pay the debt. I had the money, but it wasn't freed up in my account because my company wasn't able to set up the account properly.

It is cheaper for the medical provider to offer you a 10% to 20% discount on your bill than to pay 30% or more to a collections agency. These companies are in business to make money, and if you offer them a more economical option than a collections agency, they may take it. There have been several times when I have asked a medical facility to provide me with a discount if I paid my balance in full, and they have obliged. Sometimes it is hard to pay a balance in full if they require it, but I have had them offer interest free payments for several years, which is not a bad option if you can't afford to pay the amount in full.

I recall one medical bill being several thousand dollars and being surprised when I spoke to the medical provider and they asked me what I could afford to pay monthly. I told them I could only afford fifty dollars a month, and they were willing to work with me. However, I did end up paying the bill off early even though I probably should have taken my own advice and kept my cash in the bank and made the minimum payments to the medical provider. Collection agencies will send you mail, constantly call you, and become pests until you feel overwhelmed and want to die. People end up filing bankruptcy for small bills they could have eventually paid off by working with the medical providers, thereby keeping their good credit. So, if you are in this position and receiving those ugly red and pink letters marked "FINAL NOTICE," you should call the company right away. Again, you want to be polite to the people you speak with; it is your bill that you owe, and if they are willing to work with you, be thankful and know you are being blessed. "Just Ask" them what they can do to help you out. Most of the time, when you're talking to a human on the other end of the line, they have compassion and work with you. At least, I hope that would be the case.

How to Turn on Survival Mode If You Lose Your Job

I worked for a company in Chicago that filed a Chapter 11 bankruptcy, and I lost my job. I then had to decide what would be best for my family and what was important to me. Fortunately, my wife and children were always supportive, and together we decided to sell our home and reduce as much debt as possible to make ends meet. This meant selling anything extra, like my garden tractor, my boat, and other valuable items. I then cancelled all extra things that cost us money, such as kids' extracurricular activities. My family was able to experience the miracle of kindness once again when several people helped us out.

For example, my children loved to act and were attending a children's theatre class in Naperville, Illinois, at a place called Kidz Kabaret, and when we went to the owner to pull the children from the class because I was out of work, the owner told us not to worry about the payment for the class. It brought tears to my eyes when the owner said it was about the children, not the money. I told her I would pay her back when I could. Not too long after that, I moved on to a new job and made good on my promise. When I moved, I donated some of our furniture so that Kidz Kabaret could have them for the stage sets. In the end it became a win for both parties, and it was something I will never forget. Next time you're in Naperville, stop by Kidz Kabaret and watch some great kids act in a play.

The next event of kindness we experienced came from Dish Network, yes Dish Network. I called Dish Network to cancel my subscription to their satellite TV service, and they asked if there was anything they could do to help. At the time my payment was about $100 a month. I asked them how I could keep the equipment so that I could have it when I moved. They told me that there would be no cancelation fee and that I could sign up again free of charge when I was able to purchase their service again. The representative told me they could provide me all the channels I had, with the exception of a few special movie channels, for the price of the box rental. The payment ended up being between ten and twenty dollars a month for almost all the channels I had. This may have been a good economic decision to keep a customer on their part, but I appreciated their help. Their kindness worked for me.

After working out the Dish Network issues, I realized the Quicken computer program I used to pay my bills online was about to expire and that I would not be able to use the program to pay my bills because I needed a newer version. I had already ignored upgrading the program for at least a year because I was too frugal to pay for the update, and now my time had run out right when I lost my job. It always seems like the old saying "when it rains it pours" comes true when one is on the brink of disaster or suffering. I called Quicken and told them I had lost my job and that the version of the program I was using was about to expire and that I had a lot of bills set up on auto pay and that it would be difficult for me to manage the bills without their program. The representative was kind and said she would try to help me out. She placed me on hold for a minute or two and then said she was authorized to give me an annual subscription for the year. I was so surprised that they were willing to help me out and give me a full year upgrade for free that I secretly gave her a big kiss through the phone.

Once again, I received help in unexpected ways and was blessed with the kindness and compassion of others just by being honest and sharing my needs. People, including myself, always like to feel they are needed and are able to help other people. In small ways, these companies sold me on their products, and their customer service representatives impressed me more than anything else, and they did a great job to retain my loyalty. You can say it was not much to give a few free TV channels or allow children to be in a play, but to me it was a lot when I had so little.

"Just Ask" Yourself

- What expenses are you paying, and do you need all of the things you are paying for?
- Can you cut back your expenses and live with less so you can give more?
- Can you set up automatic payments so that you don't have to remember to pay bills?
- What are you using now that you can ask for discounts on or a better rate?
- Have you asked for any discounts to your bill providers lately?

"Just Ask" Others

- Ask for promotional offers from current providers (e.g., call your internet provider and ask for a discount or credit).
- Ask your current phone company for free stuff, like extra data, a credit, or a reduced rate.
- Ask your bank for a free set of checks or some free things you could use.
- Ask your utility providers to wave things like hazardous transport fees for propane. Ask for a cheaper rate on your utilities.
- Ask if there are any rebates for free things from your providers.

"I asked the hospital to reduce the total amount they billed me for an emergency room visit. They reduced the bill by 40% and saved me thousands of dollars."
—Jamie S., Kansas, KS

"I asked a friend's TV provider to reduce the rate for their services to help her out. They reduced her rate by over $350 a year, and she kept the same TV channels."
—Connie S., Plover, WI

"I asked my propane company for a better rate on fuel cost and to waive their hazardous shipping fees, and they saved me over $300 with a simple five-minute call."
—Julie G., Negaunee, MI

"I asked my current insurance company for a discount if I set up auto pay on my account, and they saved me $60 a year."
—Phil G., Manhattan, KS

"I asked a utility company for a general discount for being a good customer, and they gave me a $50 credit for just asking."

  —Katelyn D., Linwood, WI

"I asked a stock investment company for free trades, and they gave me $200 in free trades."

  —David D., Detroit, MI

"I asked my utility company to remove a late fee, and it saved me about $50."

  —Margaret H., Brooklyn, NY

"I called up when I got charged over $200 for a toll when traveling, and they reduced my rate to $14."

  —Lisa H., Stevens Point, WI

Chapter 3
Credit Cards

In this chapter you will learn how to pay down your credit cards, negotiate better interest rates on your current balances, and use your credit cards to get free money if you are disciplined. By understanding how credit cards work and knowing what questions to ask your providers, you will empower yourself to make better decisions that can affect your financial health. Having an understanding of your options will provide you some mental relief knowing you are in control of your own financial destiny, you have options to help you, and you can share your learned knowledge to help others as well.

Terms and Definitions

I want to lay out some basic terms and definitions so that you can understand what I am speaking about in this chapter. It's not rocket science, but the first step to fixing issues you may have is to understand what the credit card companies are saying to you. The following are some basic terms and definitions I found online at Bankrate.com.

Annual fee
> This is an automatic fee that a credit card can charge you for the benefit of having their card. Not all cards have an annual fee, but it is something to be aware of when reviewing their terms when you sign up for a credit card.

Annual percentage rate (APR)
> This is the amount of interest you will pay annually on the total amount borrowed. This applies to credit cards and any other loan, such as a car or home loan. Keep in mind that the lower the APR, the lower your monthly interest rate will be.

Balance payoff time for minimum payments
> This is the total length of time required to pay off a credit card debt if you use only minimum payments required each month and don't make any extra payments toward your principle. Therefore, the credit card company may say you will take sixty months to pay off your card if you only make minimum payments.

Credit card balance

The amount of money owed to a credit card company.

Credit card interest rate

Interest rate for your credit card based on a set APR.

Minimum payment

This is the lowest amount of payment that a credit card company will charge you each month. This is typically 1% or 2% of the balance, plus interest and other fees. Sometimes it is just a standard low rate like twenty-five dollars. Typically, they charge you whatever makes them the most money, which their terms allow. For example, this rate can be calculated by the credit card company as a percent of your current outstanding balance. Keep in mind that your monthly payment should decrease as your balance is paid down unless the credit card company is charging you a set fee. Making minimum payments can greatly increase the length of time it takes to pay off your credit cards.

Monthly payment

This is the amount of money you choose to pay each month on your credit card balance. The credit card company calculates an amount for you to pay your balance in full or the amount the credit card company will allow based on their terms for you to make a minimum payment. However, you can pay any amount between the minimum payments to paying your balance in full. The next month, the credit card company will calculate a new amount based on how much principle you may still owe.

Principle Amount

The principle is the actual balance owed, not including interest or fees. Keep in mind that if you don't pay off your credit card each month, your principle may increase or decrease depending on the amount of payment you make and if you have other charges, such as late fees or missed payments.

Credit Card Company Have You in a Chokehold?

My wife and I moved to Washington State for part-time seasonal jobs while finishing up our college degrees. During this time, money was tight, and we ended up charging most of our expenses to our credit cards. After a short time, we were up to over $10,000 in debt on our cards, and were wondering how we were going to make the next payment. As I began to look at the monthly payments on my statement along with my interest rate of 22%, I realized that making the minimum payment would take me over twenty years to pay off my debt, and the credit card company had me in a chokehold. The credit card company sent their creditors after us for their money. Also, our student loans from college had payments due each month.

At that point, I decided we must do something. I did not know what and was not sure what I could do. I knew we were not going to ruin our credit by declaring bankruptcy to solve our debt problems. There was a friend of mine in college who paid an attorney $700 to file bankruptcy for a few thousand dollars in debt. I thought it was crazy. However, I understood his desperation to do something. I decided to take my fate into my own hands and first called the credit card company and threatened, in a nice way, to change to another company who was offering me a lower rate. I was amazed that they actually were willing to lower my rate by more than 5%, even though I was only making minimum payments. Also, I was able to get them to waive a twenty dollar late fee from my last statement. This was my first experience with learning that you could ask for help.

Zero Percent Interest Rate? Read the Fine Print.

I could feel the air being sucked out of my lungs, and I was being suffocated by the credit card system. I knew we must do something more, but what could we do? We had made all the payments on time and were good customers, but we could not seem to get ahead. I started looking at the "0%" credit card offers that came in the mail soliciting us to sign up and transfer the balance from other cards.

After reading the fine print on these offers, I realized they added transfer fees, which were up-front costs similar to interest rates. You must read the fine print on "special promotions". There was a 3% up-front charge for the transfer of the money, and the 0% interest was only for a few months and then the rate jumped to a percentage that was more than my current card. This was just another way to get a consumer to jump from one credit card company to another and still keep you in their chokehold. I was confused and frustrated. It seemed like I was trapped and that even if I switched credit card companies, my rate and monthly payments were not really going to change. When things started getting tight, we ended up late on a few payments. I called up the credit card company, and they were kind enough to reverse my charges, which I thought was very nice at the time.

While speaking with them, I asked if there was anything they could do about my interest rates and that I was looking at changing credit card companies because I was being offered a credit card from another company for 12% interest, which was 10% less than they were currently charging me per month. The representative said they would not be able to do anything at the time, but I asked if I could speak with a manager. Amazingly, the manager was willing to lower my interest if we would stay with them as a cardholder. Just think, you lend someone some money, and they are faithfully paying you back an interest rate on your investment of 22%. Would you rather they give you back your money and then you get no interest from your investment, or would you rather keep making 12% interest of your investment? The company was willing to make less interest because I was a great customer and because I owed more than I could afford to pay off, so they would be getting my great interest payment for a long time, or so they thought. Unfortunately, for a while, we had to make the minimum required payment, which meant I would be in debt to them for a long time.

Wrestling to Get out of Credit Card Debt

I was tired of getting choked down by my credit card payment, and it continually reminded me of wrestling in high school when someone tried to pin me down. Every time I would try to stand, the credit card company pulled at my feet to take me back down, and they kept trying to turn me over and squeeze me until I couldn't breathe. I continually felt pinned down making the minimum payment every month, and I wanted to escape. Fortunately, I have a wonderful wife who seldom complains no matter how bad things get, and we worked together to solve our problems. With her at my side, I knew we could eventually be free.

Together, my wife and I started putting every penny extra we had into paying down the credit card. It was hard at first, and there were many times we thought we were going to fail. We did not have a lot of extra income, and it always seemed like some type of emergency would come up to take the few extra pennies we had, but we persevered. We were committed to getting out of the chokehold the credit card company had us under, and we were desperate to succeed. We did not seem to be making much progress, but over time, we were getting ahead; it just did not seem that way when you had to think about it daily.

After a year, we noticed our balance was getting to be much less and our monthly payments were shrinking. Seeing the decrease in our overall balance drove our motivation even more, and we were like sharks that smelled blood and continued to pursue a wounded fish until it was dead and eaten. You could also say we were small fish bleeding in the ocean among the sharks and were lucky and smart enough to survive the attack and escape to freedom. Yes, we were free of this debt that had been held over our heads and was suffocating us. The day we made the last payment, we had a party and cut up all our credit cards and vowed to never again get into that position. We were on our feet and were not going to let ourselves be taken down. We were victorious. The only reason we became victorious was because we were paying more than the minimum payment required each month by the credit card company. You see, if they had their choice, you would be making interest-only payments and they would have you stuck paying forever. Paying more than the interest payment each month brought down the principle amount owed. So, for example, if you borrowed $100 at an APR of 22%, you would be paying the company $22 a year in interest. So now imagine paying interest only for five years and never paying down the principle, which is the original amount borrowed. After paying $22 for five years, you would have paid the credit card company $110 in interest without ever touching your original borrowed amount. Just think if you could invest your money like this and get a 100% return on your investment over five years. That would be phenomenal.

Get Creative in Getting out of Debt

Many times you may think there are no options beyond filing for some type of personal bankruptcy to get out of debt. However, if you get creative, you can figure out a way. I had a friend who was in credit card debt and he had worked for the military and was able to secure a loan for veterans to get out of debt. Another friend was able to sell off his high-priced vehicle and downsize so that he could pay off his credit card debt. He ended up purchasing a car without payments instead of paying over $500 a month on a new truck. This allowed him to pay off a $10,000 credit card debt in just over a year. His car payments of $500 a month added up to $6,000 a year. This does not include the higher maintenance bills, higher insurance, and so on. By buying a cheaper car, he was able to have no payments, and he only kept liability insurance on his car because if it got totaled in an accident, it would not be worth much anyway. I discuss this a little more in Chapter 6.

Credit Card Companies Double Dip

Credit card companies are huge moneymakers. They not only make money off you, they also make it off every transaction. They charge retail stores a fee every time they swipe your credit card to make a charge. It is convenient to the retail store and to us as consumers, but it does make credit card companies more money. That is why some stores set a minimum purchase of five or ten dollars to use a credit card. Otherwise, the fee they pay takes up their margin and they cannot make a profit.

Some stores pay a 5% to 10% transaction fee for every credit card transaction. A 10% fee means the store loses a dime for every dollar spent at their store. It seems as if the whole world is in a chokehold by credit card companies, but, as you will see later on, maybe we're not.

Minimum Payment Warnings and Interest Increases

To be able to share a little more about the credit card chokehold I am writing about, see Figure 3.1. The key things you should look for on your statement are how long it will take to pay off the card at minimum payments and the amount of interest you will pay over that time period. Also, they will provide a "Late Payment Warning," which will show you the penalty for making a late payment along with the amount they could increase your interest. Figure 3.1 states that if I pay the minimum payment for three years, I will have paid over $169 dollars in interest on a balance of $635. The one thing they do not say is that the balance after eleven years will still not be paid off if I increase my balance and only pay $25/month. Also, my credit card states in fine print that if I am late on a payment, I will be charged a $35 late fee, and my APR will go to 29.9%. They don't show how long it will take to pay off my credit card if my interest rate goes up to 29.9% if I miss a payment.

Figure 3.1. Sample Credit Card Statment

ACCOUNT SUMMARY	
Account Number:	
Previous Balance	$5.20
Payment, Credits	-$47.98
Purchases	+$678.42
Cash Advances	$0.00
Balance Transfers	$0.00
Fees Charged	$0.00
Interest Charged	$0.00
New Balance	$635.64
Opening/Closing Date	07/25/18 - 08/24/18
Credit Access Line	$28,000
Available Credit	$27,364
Cash Access Line	$5,600
Available for Cash	$5,600
Past Due Amount	$0.00
Balance over the Credit Access Line	$0.00

PAYMENT INFORMATION	
New Balance	$635.64
Payment Due Date	09/21/18
Minimum Payment Due	$26.00

Late Payment Warning: If we do not receive your minimum payment by the date listed above, you may have to pay a late fee of up to $37.00.

Minimum Payment Warning: If you make only the minimum payment each period, you will pay more in interest and it will take you longer to pay off your balance. For example:

If you make no additional charges using this card and each month you pay...	You will pay off the balance shown on this statement in about...	And you will end up paying an estimated total of...
Only the minimum payment	3 years	$804

If you would like information about credit counseling services, call 1-866-

YOUR ACCOUNT MESSAGES

Your next AutoPayment for $635.64 will be deducted from your account and credited on your due date (previous day if your due date falls on a Saturday). Any payment or other credit posted to your account prior to your AutoPay payment being processed will be deducted from the AutoPayment amount identified above.

Based on the scenario in Figure 3.1, if I am late on a payment I will receive a late fee of $37 and my APR will be increased to 29.9%. If I only pay the minimum monthly payment, it would take me over three years—yes, three years—to pay off an original amount of $635.64, and I would have paid an estimated total of $804. To me, that is crazy.

Getting Back in the Credit Card Race

For several years I swore I would not own another credit card, until one day when speaking with a good friend of mine named Dave about credit cards, and he told me about a card he owned that paid him interest. I listened to him tell me about how he got money back from his credit card company and that they were not a burden to him. I was a little dumbfounded, but I trusted and respected my friend and drew my ear closer to the phone. One of the things that made me listen was that Dave was able to save and invest enough money to retire at age forty-five. He was able to accomplish this working an average income job that paid him about $45,000 a year. He did this by using similar principles to the ones I share in my book. He is always asking himself what his priorities are and what he really needs to be happy and content.

As several months went by, I kept thinking about what Dave had said and kept asking myself what credit card company he was using and what their interest rate was. He told me stories of getting 1–5% cash back depending on what he purchased.

I still thought it was crazy to be spending money to make a small percent in interest and get trapped with credit cards again. My wife and I were committed to staying out of credit card debt, and we were not going to get back into the race we had lost before.

One day, the light went on in my head and I had a paradigm shift regarding my belief about credit cards. Dave was not letting the credit card company use him; he was using them as his own personal checking account. What I mean by this is that he was only buying things that he intended to buy with a check or cash. He was not buying things just to buy because he could; he was buying the things he needed and would buy anyway. Then, at the end of the month when the statement came, he paid the credit card in full with no interest. Then for every dollar he spent, on things that he would have paid cash or check for anyway, he got back 1–5% in cash. Cold hard cash. I am sure the credit card companies are hating him, but he is thanking them. Just think, they send Dave a bill every month costing them money, and Dave kindly thanks them by paying his amount in full.

After thinking about Dave's thought process, I started doing some basic calculations in my head and found out that I could be "saving money" too by using a credit card company that pays you back. I just needed to decide which company had the most interest in return for my borrowing. There were and are a lot of companies that give you the options for what I call "junk rewards," such as gift items that are really not any better priced than at a store or some type of frequent flyer miles that you may never use. I used his advice and looked for rewards that had cash as the reward. Once my wife and I found a company we were willing to deal with, we got another credit card. This time, we were smarter, wiser, and not going to allow ourselves to get pinned down again. We knew that the new credit card was going to be treated just like our checking account and that we should never spend more than we could pay off from our bank account. We started out slowly and cautiously by only paying utility bills at first. Once we realized we were under control, we added more of our normal spending to our credit card charges. Thankfully, we had our Quicken computer program that linked to our bank account and offered a free bill payer that easily kept track of all our transactions on a daily basis.

Getting "Free Money" from Our Credit Card Company

Now that we had things 100% under control, we were ready to dive in full force. We began using our credit card for everything, including things we purchased for a dollar. This allowed us to keep track of our spending and also allowed us to get between 1% and 5% back on our monthly spending. It became easier and safer for us to set up our automatic payments for everything from household utilities to annual renewals of things, such as insurance. The spending was getting easier, but we still had to be aware that it would be easy to overspend on the credit card and that if we were to ever miss a payment, all our hard work would be for nothing. We kept it together and reaped the rewards of having self-control and earning free money by using the credit card on things we needed and not using it as a high-interest loan.

"Just Ask" Yourself

- Can you be disciplined enough to have a credit card?
- Can you afford to pay the high interest rates if you carry a balance?
- Can you live happy in debt?
- What example are you setting for others if you are in debt?
- What benefits are the best for you if you have a credit card?

"Just Ask" Others

- Ask credit card companies to lower your interest rates.
- Ask credit card companies for forgiveness if you are late with a payment.
- Ask your credit card company to match other credit card offers.
- Ask if there are any fees before signing up for a new credit card, especially if you are transferring balances.
- Ask if you can get a reduced rate for paying your balance in full. Yes, "Just Ask".

"Just Ask" Savings

"I asked my credit card company for free points for hotel stays, and they provided additional points."
   —Julie G., Negaunee, MI

"I asked our credit card company if they would provide me a lower interest rate if I transferred another card's balance to their account. They allowed me to consolidate my balances to one account at a rate below 10% so I could pay my cars off quicker."

—John D., Detroit, MI

"I asked for better cash points from my credit card company, and I got back over $1,000 when using my credit cards for things I already buy and paying off the statement monthly."

—Deb G., Burr Ridge, IL

Chapter 4
Clothing

In this chapter you will learn how to pick clothing trends that last, purchase end-of-season and discounted brand name clothes, and learn why it is important to have loungewear. Knowing how to purchase clothing will improve your financial destiny so you can help yourself and others, and it will teach you to ask yourself what is important to you and what type of values you want others to recognize.

Following the Trends

As a child, I liked roller skating whenever I could. All the cool kids had trendy leather skates with special wheels that allowed them to do more tricks and skate faster than me. For my birthday, I asked for a pair of roller skates and was fortunate enough to get a pair. The roller skates I received were from an inexpensive store and were made of plastic or vinyl and were very shiny. The first time I went to the rink to show off my new skates and do some tricks, I was made fun of by other kids and even some older people I respected. I can still remember them making fun of my skates and saying things like, "Don't place them skates too close to a heater; they might melt." Looking back, it doesn't seem like all that much of a bad experience, but at the time I was embarrassed and felt different than the others for being poor.

This same skating rink was where I wore designer look-alike tennis shoes that cost a few dollars compared to the ones endorsed by the stars. Kids saw the label and made fun of my shoes. I was so embarrassed that I cut the tag off the shoes that stated the brand. I believe kids still knew they were knockoffs, but it made me feel better. Looking back now, I shouldn't have cared. You have to ask yourself if following a trend is more important than teaching yourself and others that there is more to life than a trend, which is here today and gone tomorrow. It is too bad that kids make fun of others, but I was tough enough to handle ridicule most of the time, even though sometimes it still hurt.

This is why I encourage people to be polite and courteous to people when they "Just Ask". I believe in helping others, and this book is a small way of taking the time to share and help others with their finances. I want people to realize that their pennies can add up to a lot of real money. Originally, I was going to title this book, *1,000,000 pennies is $10,000* so that people could see how the pennies add up. I changed the title, but I still go into detail about this in Chapter 11. How many times do you walk down the street and see money on the ground and just ignore it? I hope that everyone who reads this book will be a little more aware of how much those pennies and nickels and dimes and quarters add up. It is our job to be prudent with our finances so that we can use some of the extra money we have to help other people.

Having a big car or fancy house and a lot of material things may bring some people value, but it's only a very shallow value that is not rooted in love. If you truly want to bring value to others, you need to help them by being a living example of a caring and financially responsible person. I look at Warren Buffet as a good example of simple living because he comes across as a humble person who wants to help others. Warren Buffett and other extremely successful people tend to avoid trends and stick to more classic looks that never go out of style. Even Steve Jobs created a uniform for himself and help set the trend that there is no trend.

Buying Quality Clothing Can Save You Money

Over the years I have learned that having good quality clothing can be less expensive than having clothes of lesser quality. The cost up-front may be more for the quality product, but it will pay for itself in the long run. For example, if you buy a cheaper pair of jeans for your child, but they tear easily, did you truly save money?

When you are buying things like shoes, consider the long-term impact they will have on your body. For example, if you buy a cheap pair of running shoes, could that impact your knees and back and end up causing you to wear out your joints or needing medical care?

Quality Clothing Can Cost Less Than Trendy Name Brands

Some jeans cost more money than a quality pair of dress pants, and a trendy name brand T-shirt may cost more than a quality dress shirt. The cost you're going to pay depends on a few things: the brand; the retailer; the type and quality of the clothing; and the season. When I was younger many kids I knew had designer jeans that cost a lot of money. When I asked my father to take me shopping for a pair of jeans like theirs, he convinced me to buy a no-name brand. I was sure the push was because the pants I bought were half the price of the designer clothing, and my dad did not want to let me know that he was tight on money. All I remember was that my "friends" made fun of my jeans. Again, it hurt, but it did teach me that you don't always get what the other kids have, and that is perfectly acceptable. If we end up getting everything we want as children, will we work as hard for other things in life? The jeans my father purchased for me may have been half the price, but they held up better than the designer jeans because the denim material was a better quality.

Not all high-end brands are the best. I once purchased a high-end dress shirt with all the trendy logos on it. I hated the shirt because it was made out of such a thin material that would always wrinkle no matter how much I ironed it. It cost me more time and effort to get it ready for work than my other shirts. Also, minutes into my commute, it looked like I hadn't ironed it at all. Remember that good quality does not always mean the most expensive.

Clothing Is Just a Tool

I eventually realized that clothing is only a tool that protects your body from the elements. Remember my friend Dave from Chapter 3? The one who retired at age forty-five? He purchases most of his clothing from thrift stores. Of course, if buying cheap clothes was the only thing we needed to do to get us to retirement, we could all be retired at forty-five by following the principles in this chapter. However, it does take more than just buying on the cheap; it takes discipline and dedication.

Discount Clothing

My first experience with purchasing quality clothes for a good price was when I bought a pair of cowboy boots in Washington on clearance at a local shopping mall. The boots were a hundred dollars, and I was able to purchase them for less than twenty dollars on clearance by asking the clerk for the best clearance price. When I saw the boots and the price the clerk gave me, I thought someone clearly mislabeled them. The clerk shared that the boots were being discontinued to make room for a newer style. After getting such a great deal, I went to the clothing section in the same store and was able to find dress pants on clearance for seven dollars a pair, discounted from forty dollars. They were the same brand and type I normally purchased for much more.

How could these prices be so good? The answer was simple: people want new styles. The store was clearing out last season's items to make way for the next season and the more trendy styles. In looking at the clearance or bargain areas over the years, I saved a lot of money. However, I did learn that not every clearance item was truly a bargain. Sometimes the item was only marked down a small percent. Also, I did find that when something was a great deal, I overspent. For example, when I found my favorite dress pants on sale, I would buy several pairs of them until I had about twelve new pairs in my closet. I then asked myself, when is enough is enough? The answer to my question was simple: a great deal is not a great deal if you don't need the item. So make sure you continue to "Just Ask" yourself if you really need the item on sale or if you are just purchasing it because it is a great buy.

Shop Adult and Children Sections

My son, who is fairly skinny for being in his late teens, was able to go to the kids' section in a store and buy an NFL jersey that was priced at $112 for only $12 on clearance. After some additional discounts, it came out to just over $9. My son would usually wear a small men's size, so sometimes he can find an extra large size in a kids' or juniors' section that fits him. My wife does the same thing by checking out the girls' section because she normally wears a petite size, so many times kid sizes will fit her great. Don't be afraid to check out other sections to be creative in your shopping, including girls shopping boys sections and vice versa. You never know what you may find.

End-of-Season Clothes

As I shared before, the clearance items I was purchasing were end-of-season or discontinued and were being marked down to make way for the next season's items. After figuring this out, a light bulb when on in my head, and I decided to save money by planning ahead for each season and stocking up on the clearance items for the next season. In a couple of seasons of planning, I was able to have a closet full of the "best" name brand clothing one could imagine at pennies on the dollar for most of the items. The twelve pairs of pants I had purchased were still brand new with tags on them several years later. The only thing was that over time the pants seemed to shrink a little in my closet, and they were fitting tighter around my waist. OK, maybe it was just that I was getting older and my metabolism was changing. I also think my wife's great cooking might have had something to do with it. Bottom line: don't spend just because something is on sale.

Before you go out shopping you should "Just Ask" yourself if you're getting an item you can get a lot of use out of or if you'll be giving it away the following season because it is out of style. If you ask yourself what colors or styles have been around a long time and are still trendy and you follow that lead, you will most likely purchase clothing that will last and be in style for years to come. Patterns and trends are always changing, so stick with basic, solid colors, and you will be good to go for a long time. You don't have to change all your clothing at once. You can still buy things that go out of style each season, but you need to ask yourself before each purchase if you want to have things that will last and save you money or if you want to spend your money chasing trends that you can never keep up with.

Many of my friends buy clothing a little larger for their children so that they can get more use out of them before they outgrow them. Then they share the clothing with others as hand-me-downs or donate them to a store.

Remember that a great deal on an item you can't use is no deal at all; it is just a waste of money and time. Don't clutter your closet and home with great deals that you may never use. If you plan ahead and look for a specific item, similar to how I shop for a car (see Chapter 6), then you are more likely to not purchase too much stuff. Again, be careful to only buy what you need and not to tie up all your cash in things that just hang in your closet or sit on a shelf.

Loungewear

Changing your clothes when you get home can prolong the life of your going out clothes. Growing up, I remember my mother telling me to change into my play clothes before going outside. She was absolutely correct in stating this. We should all learn from this and consider having some loungewear. They may be just a pair of sweatpants and a T-shirt, but having a set of comfortable clothes to lounge around the house can save wear and tear on your good clothes. I like to work in the shop on vehicles and do other mechanical things, so having clothes that I can get oil and grease on saves me a lot of money. I have several old dress shirts I use while cutting the lawn. They work great because they have long sleeves and help me keep the dirt, bugs, and sun off my skin. If a sleeve gets torn, it becomes a short-sleeve shirt with a simple cut of my scissors. If you have a good seamster in your family, that damaged shirt may turn into a new short-sleeve shirt that can be used outside the home. You just have to ask yourself how you can use your creativity to make practical decisions that help the environment, help save you money, and meet your clothing needs.

Beyond Clothes

One Christmas season I was able to buy all the ornaments and lights for the next few seasons by shopping the clearance sales at the local stores. Most of the prices were marked down at least 75%. I also bought a new watch for pennies on the dollar because it came in Christmas packaging. Ask yourself if you can use a seasonal item on clearance to meet your needs all year long. During this same trip, I bought several packages of small Christmas light bulbs that were the same as the night-light bulbs I needed, and they were only 10% of the cost of the same item in the lighting aisle. The only difference was that there were ten in a package compared to only two in a pack in the lighting aisle. The two light bulbs in the lighting aisle were two dollars for the pack of two bulbs and the ten pack was only a dime. Yes, only a dime for ten bulbs or a penny a piece compared to a dollar per bulb. That is 99% of the cost of the non-clearance bulbs. Think outside the box, especial fancy seasonal boxes, during seasonal clearance time.

Practice Each Season

If you want to practice this technique, I recommend that you start to watch your local department stores for end-of-season clearances and discontinued items. You can "Just Ask" the clerk for the schedule of when they start to clear out their items for the season. In general, you can expect winter clothing to be cleared out from the middle to end of winter; spring clothes are cleared out in late spring; and summer clothes are cleared out mid- to late summer. You've seen the after-Christmas sales on holiday decorations and lighting. Just think of other items in the same way. Most items end up being updated, and you can get a discontinued model for a lot less than the current models.

"Just Ask" yourself before you buy electronics, toys, clothing, cars, bikes, sporting equipment, and so on if you need the latest model or if you can wait for the clearance sale on last year's model. The greatest challenge in buying items on clearance is planning ahead. If you end up having to buy an item in the same season as you want to use it, plan on paying top dollar for the item. For example, if you want to buy a baseball glove in the spring and early summer, you will most likely pay top dollar, whereas if you buy it in the fall, you should be able to get a good glove on sale. In the end, you have to make a choice on what you value more: the savings or having the most current item on the market. If you can afford to spend the extra money, feel free to spend a lot of the extra money you have because you are helping the economy. However, for those people who value saving money more than the glory of having the most current items, I'll see you in the clearance aisle.

"Just Ask" Yourself

- What examples are you setting?
- Can you buy classic pieces for the long run?
- Do you need to have the latest trends?
- Are you OK with being your own trendsetter?
- Can you plan ahead to save money in the long term?

"Just Ask" Others

- Ask for extra savings if you buy a lot of clearance items.
- Ask stores to discount discontinued models that meet your needs.
- Ask stores when they plan to clear out their seasonal items.
- Ask for coupons or any other savings items.
- Ask the clerk for a discount.

"Just Ask" Savings

"I asked the store for an additional discount when buying clearance items, and they gave me 30% more off my bill. I saved over $500 on a $600 purchase for brand new clothes."
—Frank W., Marquette, MI

"I ask for discounts on new clothing when I buy more than one item, and many times I have gotten a reduced rate from 10 to 50% depending on what I am buying."
—Heidi M., East Point, MI

"I ask the salesperson for a savings coupon when I don't get them in the mail. They have given me the discounts numerous times, saving me over $500 a year on all our family's clothing."
—Clay N., Naperville, IL

"I asked a company that sells high-end clothing to replace a defective piece of clothing that was worth over $100, and they replaced it, no questions asked."

—Lilian H., Roseville, MI

"I asked for a discount on a new pair of pants that had a loose snap. I saved $30, and I fixed the issue myself for pennies."

—Rose M., Homestead, FL

Chapter 5
Saving on Groceries

In this chapter you will learn about the cost of groceries for a family, using coupons, meal planning, and more. By planning your grocery shopping trips, you will improve your finances and your health.

Grocery Costs

Groceries can be one of the most expensive parts of a family budget. In fact, the US Department of Agriculture says that feeding a family of four a healthy diet can cost as much as $289 a week. That ends up being $15,028 a year. The US Census Bureau in 2017 stated the average household income is $60,336. The tax rate in 2018 for people earning between $38,701 to $82,500 is 22%. If your household income is $57,617, after paying 22% in taxes ($12,676), your take-home pay would be $44,941. If you pay $15,028 a year in groceries for a family of four, you will have $29,913 left for all your other bills such as your mortgage, heating, vehicle, fuel, clothing, and so on. In the end, you will be lucky to have a few thousand dollars left for purchasing underwear and socks, as you will see in Table 5.1. Keep in mind that not every family has an income level of over $50,000 and may have much less.

The best way I have found to save money buying groceries is simple: plan, plan, plan, plan. Yes, you should plan to save money by buying only what you need. We have all heard about the great deals out there and people getting free stuff all the time. Well, most of the time, it is not really free. For example, if you buy twenty dollars' worth of a certain brand of product, you may get one of their other products free. This is a way to give you a discount to try other items they sell in hopes that you will buy more of the new product later. Many times coupons are meant to get people to try new items or to promote a seasonal product. This may leave the saver with products that they would not normally buy.

Table 5.1. Chart of average yearly expenses for a family of four in the US

Income[1]	$57,617
Federal taxes[2]	$12,676
Groceries[3]	$15,028
Mortgage[4]	$12,360
Utilities (gas, electric, water, trash)[5]	$1,800
Phone, cable, and internet[6]	$900
Automobile[7]	$8,558
Average annual out-of-pocket healthcare expenses for a family of four as of 2017[8]	$4,704
Average insurance premium payment for a family of four as of 2017[9]	$7,674
Remaining balance for other expenses	**($6,083)**

[1] Average US income according to the US Census Bureau

[2] Tax amount based on 2018 Federal government tax rate at 22%

[3] US Department of Agricultural grocery cost for eating healthy for a family of four

[4] The median monthly mortgage payment for US homeowners is $1,030, according to the latest American Housing Survey from the US Census Bureau.

[5] Utilities based on a total combined rate of $150 month average for water, electric, and gas

[6] Phone, cable, and internet based on a total of $75 month

[7] AAA 2016 driving costs estimate of a small sedan at 15,000 miles a year

[8-9] Based on the annual Milliman Medical Index for September 2017

Reward Yourself for Things You Would Buy Anyway

Many stores offer reward cards for saving money when shopping. Read the terms of the agreement. Some companies track your shopping habits and sell your information to other companies so that they can solicit you for sales. Reward cards go well beyond grocery shopping, so "Just Ask" yourself what type of items you could get a reward card for that may benefit you for something you would buy anyway.

I always use a reward card for my fuel purchases, which may only give me a free coffee or donut, but it doesn't cost me anything. I like to buy the $1.00 coffee from one of my favorite restaurants, and if I use their reward system, I can get a free coffee or specialty drink for every five purchases I make. So I buy my five coffees and then use the free one to reward myself with a specialty coffee, which would be over four dollars. So I am earning a 20% to 40% savings, depending on the expense of the free coffee I chose, on something I would buy anyway.

Pick what works for your spending habits and start saving money or earning free items that you were going to buy anyway. Just reward yourself.

Check Your Cupboards, Refrigerator, and Freezer
Plan what you need based on what you already have so that you only buy what you need for the week. Try to use up all the items in your pantry so you don't get stuck with expired products buried in the back of your cupboards that are never used. See what you have and plan meals accordingly. This way you won't have expired or spoiled goods in the pantry, and you will be more efficient and less likely to want to choose pre-made meals, which aren't healthy and could cost you more in medical bills in the long run.

Will You Make the List?
Write down exactly what you need to buy and stick to the list. Many times when you go to the grocery store without planning, you will buy much more than you originally intended. Especially if you grab the local flyer and see all those great sale items you "must" have. If you plan for success and know what you need, you will be able to manage your spending much better and won't get as tempted to buy the items that catch your eye just because they are on sale.

Don't Let Being Hungry Make You Poor
If you go to the store when you are hungry, you are apt to purchase more food than if you go when you are not hungry. Therefore, if you plan your trip efficiently and have a list, you will not be as tempted to purchase extra snacking foods, such as ice cream and cookies. I am fortunate in that my wife likes to do the shopping, and I rarely need to shop for our groceries. This prevents me from buying a lot of snack foods and other costly items I really do not need.

Get Back to the Basics
If you buy flour, you can make bread, pancakes, waffles, pizza crust, pie crusts, and more. If you buy potatoes, you can make baked potatoes, mashed potatoes, potato pancakes, or add them to pot roast. A bag of flour is just a few dollars and can create so

many items. Just think, you can buy some pre-made frozen waffles or pancakes and pay several dollars for a couple servings, or you can buy the ingredients for much less and have many more servings.

Portion Your Meals

Make enough food for your meal by portioning out what is needed. This will prevent you from having extra food that you do not eat and ends up in the trash. If you do make extra, you can freeze or refrigerate it for a later meal. This will save you a lot of money by enabling you to do a large batch with little more work than it takes to make a smaller batch. If you bought flour at the store and decide to make pancakes, you can make extra and store them in a zipper bag in the freezer. The clean-up will be the same whether you make a small batch or a larger batch.

Generally, protein is going to be the main driver when shopping at a store. If one store has chicken breast for 50% of the price of other stores and it is on your list, this will most likely be the store to shop at that week.

Momma Used Coupons, Why Can't You?

My mother would wait for the local supermarket to have triple coupons before she would buy groceries. Sometimes she would even be able to use a coupon for a whole different category or a different store. For example, she could give the clerk some cereal coupons but buy bread, and they would still take the coupons. I guess this was the first time I heard her "Just Ask." Sometimes the store would take them, and other times they might not. These days it seems a lot more rigid than in her buying days with all the electronic controls. At my young age of ten, it did not seem like the right thing to do from a moral or ethical standpoint, but as I grew older and became a teenager it appeared to be acceptable. She certainly was creative! I also remember the days when she would save coupons and "Just Ask" the sales clerk if they could take extra coupons by letting her use more and she would give them some of her extra coupons so the clerk could save some money too. With our current technology and barcode system, this may not work, but it shares the thought of Just Asking.

Stick to the Outside

The outer aisles usually have the basics foods—items such as fruits, vegetables, breads, meats, eggs, milk, and butter—which can be used to make many other items or meals. Also, they are generally the healthiest and least unprocessed foods. Keep in mind that the aisle items are generally cheaper priced than buying pre-made or processed meals, and they can last for several meals.

Track Your Spending

Track your expenses on a monthly basis so that you can budget what to spend each month. This sounds simple, which it is, but you have to be able to keep track of what you spend if you want to track your progress and save money. Anytime you track something, it automatically allows you to think about the results and what you are doing. If you had an unlimited budget and never had to track expenses, I guarantee you would spend more than if you tracked your expenses.

Spend more time at home preparing simple meals rather than going out to eat. This will save you a ton of money and will allow you to spend more time with your family. Sometimes it takes a little while, but kids will eventually buy into your program, especially if you let them choose.

If you allow your kids to choose dinner once in a while using what you have in the fridge, it will make them feel special and want to help. Anytime you can get your children to buy into your program, you will see that they become more excited to help get the results. Keep it simple for them and make some basic rules. For example, dinner must have one protein, a vegetable, fruit, and, of course, a dessert. Doing this trains your children to be more responsible and resourceful when they are older.

"Just Ask" Yourself

- Will buying cheap groceries cost you more for medical bills in the long run and affect your health?
- What type of example are you setting for others by what you buy for groceries?
- Can you afford to skip the coupons, or is your time more valuable?
- Can you buy nutritious foods for cheaper than other highly processed foods?
- How can you save time by planning meals ahead for the week and making larger batches when cooking?
- Can you eat at home more often to save money and improve your health?

"Just Ask" Others

- Ask the stores for coupons on the items you are buying.
- Ask the store if they will match their competitor's sale prices.
- Ask the store if they will discount dented boxes or slightly bruised vegetables or fruits.
- Ask if the store will take different coupons for similar items or if they can take an expired coupon.
- Ask if you can get a discount for items of which you buy large quantities.
- Ask friends who like to collect coupons if they can save some for the items you buy.

"Just Ask" Savings

"I don't usually have in-store coupons, so I ask the store clerk for their coupons when I go to the grocery store to shop. They usually give me coupons, and it has saved me over $400 in a year."
   —Ann N., Naperville, IL

"I asked the cashier if I could use a competitor's store coupon and saved over $50 on a grocery bill."
   —Les S, Chicago, IL

"I ask the grocery store for discounts on items if they are bruised or damaged yet fully edible and functional."
   —Van H., Seattle, WA

"A friend asked the grocery store if they could have a discount when buying items for charitable organizations, such as for turkey baskets at Thanksgiving, and the store reduced their cost and gave them some additional free items to help with the baskets."
   —Jenny J., San Francisco, CA

"I went shopping with a friend who saves coupons, and we filled our cart with over $300 in groceries and got money back after shopping. Yes, we got our groceries free and got money back. I was able to do this by just asking my friend who knows the best ways to save money shopping."
   —Haddy J., Omaha, NE

Chapter 6
Buying a Car

Buying an automobile can be an exciting adventure. However, sometimes the excitement can lead to buyer's remorse. After you have made your car purchase, it can be easy to regret the purchase as you make large payments each month and the car continues to depreciate. Before you know it, you are "upside down" in the value of your car versus what you owe. Meaning that you have a car worth less than what you owe on it. There are several ways to avoid this happening to you. In this chapter you will learn about buying a new car, buying a used car, and leasing a car. You will also learn when you should walk away from a purchase.

Never Buy a New Car
From a depreciation standpoint, you are better off buying a used car than buying a new car. Never buy a new car unless you have so much money that you can start a fire with $100 bills. If you buy a new car and only keep it a year or two, you are going to be selling it or trading it in for less than what you paid. No matter how well you take care of it or how few miles are on it, it will be worth thousands less than the day you bought it. Also, you will have paid your state taxes and licensing fees, which most likely add thousands more to the overall cost associated with owning a vehicle.

Therefore, let's say you bought a $10,000 car in a state with a 7% sales tax rate and a $300 fee for licensing and registration. The sales tax would end up being $700. So far, you've spent an additional $1,000 on the new car. Now you have a total of $11,000 paid for the great "new vehicle". Also, let's say you financed the whole car for thirty-six months with a low rate of 5%, so now you have a monthly payment of about $330 with an average of $39.23 of the payment going to interest. By the end of one year, you will have paid an additional $470.76 in interest to the loan company, and you have a grand total of $11,470.76 invested in your new beauty. Now let's say that a year later you decide to sell the car because a new one came out with some "better options". If you end up selling the car for only $7,500.00, which is realistic, you will have lost $3,470.76

in one year just off the sale of the car. In one year you paid out in $3,960 in finance payments with only $3,489.24 going to the principle payment and $470.76 going toward interest. Therefore, when you close on the sale of your car, you will owe an additional $10.76 to the loan company. This is just one example of how quickly and easily you can be "upside down" with a car by owing more than it is worth. Now if you go to buy a new car for the same price, you will be back in the same situation where you are setting yourself up to lose even more money.

Paying for Status Symbol
In summary if you buy a new car, you will lose money. "Just Ask" yourself how much money can you afford to lose. You can self-justify buying a new car by saying you will keep it for many years, you got 0% financing, it was a great deal, and so on. However, keep in mind that a vehicle is just a mode of transportation whose function is to take you to places where you can make more money. To some people a vehicle is a status symbol. You need to decide if you would rather have a status symbol or more money in your pocket toward your retirement and other things you might find more valuable.

There's nothing wrong with buying a new vehicle if a person can afford it, and it does help support the economy. Every person needs to look at their own situation and decide what is best. So be prudent in your review and decision-making, and try to decide based on your financial situation and not on the emotion of going to a dealership and having a salesperson talk you into buying a car you don't need.

Do You Have Enough Self Control?
If you don't have much self-control, it's best not to go to a dealership and get approached by a salesperson when their job is to make you think you need a car and then take advantage of the opportunity that you're there. The best way to look for a vehicle and comparison shop is to know exactly what you want and then do a lot of your research online. Before you go to a car lot, make sure you know exactly what you're willing to negotiate for and the type of vehicle you want. Also, prepare yourself to "Just Ask" a lot of questions. For example, if you go to a car dealership looking at one make and model of the vehicle and then they tell you that—for just a little bit more—you can

buy their flagship vehicle. It has more options, and it's only five grand more. You may get talked into buying that vehicle even though you have not done research on it.

For most people, buying a vehicle is the second most expensive purchase they ever make—their home being the most expensive. Yet many people walk into a dealership not knowing what they want or need and let the salesperson sell them what they want to sell. The salesperson makes the most money and gets the most incentives. I'm not saying that every dealership or salesperson is like that, but you need to be wary. You need to hold everyone accountable, and you should do your own research so you can walk away a happy customer, even if you're buying a new car.

When you buy a vehicle, you should always look to buy the most economical one possible to meet your needs. If you are a salesperson and you know you will be driving a lot, then comfort and gas mileage may be key areas to focus on. If you buy a car that gets ten miles per gallon, you'll be spending twice as much on fuel than if you had purchased a car that gets twenty miles per gallon.

"Just Ask" for Special Incentives

One other way to save money when negotiating with a dealer is to "Just Ask" if they can throw in other incentives, such as free oil changes, maintenance, or special coverage on your vehicle. A lot of times those are some of the easiest things to negotiate with the dealership. However, this can only be done if you "Just Ask" the question. At the very least, you should "Just Ask" the salesperson if there are any discounts or a better rate they can give you. If you are not comfortable doing this, bring a friend you trust who can help you negotiate. This works really well because the person helping may not have any emotional attachment to the vehicle and will be looking out for your best interest.

If you have done your research and buy only what you know you want and need, you will have car values already in your mind to know if you're getting a good deal or a bad deal from the dealership. If you ever become uncomfortable, it doesn't hurt to walk away from the dealer. Salespeople can become very pushy. Remember, there will always be another "perfect car".

Buying a Used Vehicle

When buying a used vehicle, decide what you need first and then begin your search. Start with the most cost-effective and fuel-efficient vehicle possible that will meet your overall needs. The larger the vehicle, generally, the more expensive the parts, maintenance, and fuel will be. Also, generally, the larger the vehicle, the more expensive it would typically cost to purchase because more materials are used in manufacturing.

If you buy a vehicle that meets your needs but is on the smaller side, tires, fuel, repairs, and even oil changes will be less expensive than a larger car. Knowing what type of vehicle you want will make you a better negotiator. The salesperson will not be able to talk you into a vehicle that does not meet your needs. Many people go to the car lot or dealership not knowing what they want, the options they want, or the price they want. Then, after about fifteen minutes, the great salesperson has sold them "exactly" what they think they need, and it is at the top of their price range or even higher because they qualify for financing. This all happens because the salesperson asked you all the questions and led you down the path they wanted to go instead of you asking the questions that lead where you want to end up.

Buying from a No-Haggle Dealership

Some dealerships, such as CarMax, offer a no-haggle price on used cars. You can either buy the car at the price they are offering or go somewhere else. You can look at this as good or bad depending on what you are comfortable with when purchasing a vehicle. "Just Ask" yourself if it is worth not having to negotiate for a price. If you are not comfortable dealing with people, especially pushy salespeople, this may be an option for you.

What I have noticed is that companies that have no-haggle pricing tend to be fair about the vehicle prices. Also, they generally have good reputations for getting quality vehicles with a good history, and they back their vehicles with their reputation. Typically they will have a warranty on your purchase as well. I once purchased a vehicle from CarMax prior to seeing it. I knew the exact vehicle I wanted down to the color, and they had it in stock, only it was at another location that was not near me. After I paid for the vehicle, the car arrived a few days later. It had everything as described, except the tow hitch, which was listed on the sales sheet. I brought this to their attention, and they made good on the deal, no questions asked.

Buying for Sale by Owner

I have been practicing a different approach in car buying over the last twenty years, and it has served me very well. However, I must warn you that you must be patient and willing to walk away from some deals. Also, you will need to have knowledge of car values and vehicle mechanics or a good, reliable mechanic or shop to check out the vehicle for you if you are not able to evaluate it effectively yourself.

I have been buying primarily For Sale by Owner (FSBO) my whole life, and I have only had experience with buying one new vehicle. Yes, I can afford to buy new vehicles, but I find my money serves me better appreciating in investments than buying something I am sure to lose money on. Buying a new vehicle is like dumping money down a hole. Even if the car I owned was worth only a thousand dollars and my house was worth close to a million dollars, I wouldn't care that my neighbors drove "prestige" type vehicles.

The reason car price is not as important is because cars generally depreciate and homes appreciate. Not that anyone needs a million-dollar house, but there might be reasons why you would buy one if you could profit from it. Those reasons are discussed in Chapter 8. There are advantages to having vehicles that are older and not too complicated. For example, if you are in the dating scene, and you drive a used older car, you will generally be dating people who care more about you than the car you own or the house you live in. Insurance will be cheaper on an older used car. Also, if someone at the shopping center happens to back into your car or scratches it with a shopping cart, you might not feel like it is the end of the world. Also, parts are cheaper and easier to come by. A vehicle that is dependable and reliable does not have to look like a diamond, but it can still be your goldmine.

Find Your Own Strategy

My strategy is to find the type, make, and model of car I want to purchase along with the exact package options. Then I spend some time looking online for cars in about a three- to six-year-old range under a hundred thousand miles. Once I start to get a feel for their value, I narrow my search down even further and begin to determine what I am willing to pay. This is where patience will be needed.

Once I know the car or truck I want, I research the trade-in value and the private party value online. I always target buying a car at or below the trade-in value, which is not always easy to do. However if one is patient, it can be done. I use the theory that if I buy a car for the trade-in value, I can usually have enough value in the car after two years of normal use to still sell it and not lose money, providing that it is still in the same condition as when I purchased it. In fact, there have been times when I bought a car for trade-in value and sold the car for more than I paid for it two years later. I then bought another car at an even better value that was newer and had fewer miles on it. This may sound easy, but there are always risks with this process. You need to find your own strategy by knowing your needs, your strengths, and the value of your time and money. Once you decide and develop your strategy, you will need to make sure that the car you are buying is in good mechanical condition. For the novice, I recommend that you take it to a dealer and pay to have the car inspected before purchase once you think you have the right vehicle. This may cost you a couple hundred dollars, but it could avoid a mistake worth several thousands of dollars if you find a major problem.

When I was younger, I went to look at a car that a person advertised as having had one owner and being in great condition. It was only a few years old. The price seemed great, and I was excited to go and see it. I set up a time with the owner and drove two and a half hours on a snowy night with my family to see the car. When I was about halfway there, the guy called me to say that he had incorrectly told me the year of the car and that it was actually a year older than he mentioned, but that he wanted to call me to make sure I knew before I drove all that way. I thought that we should still see the car being we were already over halfway there. I arrived at the guy's house, and he invited me in to his nice home and I met his pregnant wife. Also, I saw a Mercedes in the driveway and assumed this guy had a lot of money and that he was selling because he did not need the car. He let me take the car for a short drive with him and we went onto the highway for about a mile. He seemed to want to keep the distance short, which I thought was because of the snow storm. While driving the car, I could tell that there was some type of steering or braking issue. I brought it up to him, but he did not recall it having any issues. Then we were talking and something he said made me question if he was the original owner. I then asked his wife if he was really the original owner, and she looked at me for a moment and then said yes.

I negotiated with them and spent over an hour looking at the car. I ended up negotiating the best price I could while my family was stuck in our truck all that time and I was feeling hurried to make a decision. I ended up giving them thousands of dollars in cash for a vehicle I would very shortly regret purchasing. We signed the paperwork and I was off. My wife drove the new car back and I drove the truck. We stopped after leaving his home and filled up the gas tank. About thirty minutes into the drive, the check engine light went on and that was the start of many problems I would have with that car. I called the guy right back, and he said that it must have been because we did not put premium gas in the car. We thought that could make sense, but then I looked online when we got home, and learned that the car should not take premium. I then took it to a dealer, and they shared the bad news that the engine must be replaced. They mentioned that thicker oil and not driving very far could be why the check engine light was not on when we tested it. Also, the front end problem ended up being a complete rebuild for me on all the steering and suspension along with the brakes.

When I called the guy back, he would not answer any questions. I then decided to look up the history on the car, which I should have done before I purchased, and found out that this guy was not the original owner. There was nothing I could do because I bought the car "as is". This was a real learning experience, which cost me several thousands of dollars. Please take the time to take a car to a mechanic and check it out if you are not comfortable doing it yourself. If the owner is not interested in allowing you to do this, you should not buy the car from them. Even if they are your friend, you should get a professional opinion, which will make you both feel better. If something goes wrong later on down the line, you can feel confident that neither one of you knew about any issues related to the car, and your friendship will remain intact.

Leasing a Car

People often lease vehicles because they want to have a newer, maintenance-free car. Also, they like to lease vehicles because the lease rate is often cheaper than a payment rate to purchase the car. However, people make a lot of mistakes when leasing cars, and they don't build up any asset value at all because the car has to be turned back in after a period of time. Therefore, no money goes into the principal value of the car. A lot of times people don't ask about the details of the contract or read the fine print, which lists all the additional costs for any little thing wrong with the vehicle and any additional mileage on the vehicle.

Dealers offer cheap lease payments every month; however, they will want a large amount of money up front to start the lease. All you are doing is paying a portion of the car lease. Most of the suggestions I have heard from financial people is that a consumer should not pay more than $2,000 up-front on a lease. It's best to put nothing down on a lease when possible. That way the lessee could use the money to help make the monthly payments, and if by chance the vehicle were to be in an accident in the first few months, they don't lose a large down payment

If an accident were to occur a little bit further down the road in the lease, insurance companies cover the value of the car, not what you owe on it. Therefore, it will be your obligation to pay the remainder. Additional gap insurance is available to cover the amount. It would be an additional premium for you, so you would have to determine if that makes sense for you. Sometimes the dealer will offer that type of insurance with their lease; "**Just Ask**".

Time Can Eat Your Lease Saving

If you look at the overall cost of leasing a car, you will find that if you lease cars over ten years, the cost will likely exceed the purchase price of a new car and cost a lot more than buying a used car. Many lease periods range from two to three years. There are longer periods, but if you were to get involved with a longer period, you must keep in mind that there could be more maintenance repairs because the bumper-to-bumper warranty and coverage generally wears off around three years. So, make sure you understand the maintenance and repair guidelines you're committing to within your contract.

If you underestimate the mileage that you'll be driving, you could pay anywhere from ten to twenty-five cents per mile on average above and beyond what you said you would drive. Therefore, it's important that you give a good estimate of what you want in the lease contract for mileage. Most contracts are usually between 10,000 and 15,000 miles. So imagine if you sign up for a lease at 10,000 miles a year and it's for three years, and every year you end up driving 15,000 miles instead. At the end of your term you'll have driven an additional 5,000 miles above and beyond the lease. At twenty-five cents a mile for 5,000 miles, an additional $1,250 will be due at the end of your lease, and you'll have no trade-in value to buy another car.

Additionally, when leasing a vehicle, the dealership will require you to maintain full coverage on the vehicle. "Just Ask" yourself what vehicle you need. Once you decide what your needs are, you can start to look up insurance rates.

What Is Your Trade-In Value?

Make sure you get the full trade-in value of your car before you tell the car salesperson you're interested in leasing. Otherwise, the salesperson could use that information and knowledge to steer you in the direction of a deal that will make him the most money. Don't allow the salesperson to have a primary focus on the amount you want to pay per month. A salesperson who is only focused on the amount you pay is interested in making sure you pay as much as possible on the lease to make the company more money. Let them come up with the amount for the type of vehicle you want. If you find a deal online during your research that appears to be better, "Just Ask" if they can match the price. This works the same whenever you buy something. I think you're getting the point that every time you go to purchase something, you should "Just Ask".

"Just Ask" Yourself

- Can you afford the depreciation of buying a new car?
- Can you afford to go into debt to purchase a new car?
- Can you live happy in debt?
- Ask yourself if you need a new car to help you feel that you are valuable as a person?
- Does the new warranty bring you enough piece of mind to offset the stress of the debt?
- What could you do with the extra money if you bought a car and you could pay cash?
- Ask yourself what car you can get that meets your driving needs and does not break the bank.
- Ask if you have time to be patient to find the right vehicle at the right price.

"Just Ask" Others

- Ask the dealer for special deals, like no interest payments, or discounts if you pay cash.
- Ask at least three times for a better price when negotiating with a dealer.

- Ask for free things like oil changes, floor mats, and other accessories when you are at the end of the negotiations.
- Ask for extra free miles on a lease vehicle if you know you will drive more than the standard lease terms.
- Ask for more money on your vehicle trade-in value than what they originally offer.
- Ask for better interest rates or terms when you finance.
- Ask for a couple more spare keys or key fobs from the dealer. These can cost up to $250/each.
- Ask for the ancillary charges in the contract, such as paperwork fees, to be waived.

"Just Ask" Savings

"I asked for better rates from a dealer to purchase a car, and they reduced their price by thousands when I offered to pay cash."
   —Elizabeth H., Virginia Beach, VA

"I asked a dealer to fix some scratches I found on my vehicle after I purchased it, and they repainted the panel for free."
   —Frank W., Marquette, MI

"I asked for more mileage on a lease vehicle for the same price, and they extended my yearly miles from 10,000 to 15,000 for the same monthly fee."
   —Scott M., Roseville, MI

"I asked a friend to sell me their vehicle for trade-in value rather than trade it into a dealer. I purchased it, drove it for two years, and sold it for more than I paid for the vehicle. I got a free vehicle for two years and made money at the end."
   —John D., Wausau, WI

Chapter 7
Selling a Car

In this chapter you will learn how to determine your car's value, how to sell by owner, how to prep your vehicle for sale, how to sell to a dealership, and how to evaluate your time value. Also in the chapter you will learn the questions to "Just Ask" to save money.

What's It Worth?

You need to know what your car is worth if you decide to sell it. You can often look up the value of your car by checking out websites that list the values of used cars, such as KBB.com (Kelly Blue Book) or Nadaguides.com (Nada Guides). Go to JustAskTheBook.Com to find more information. Also, you can look up the price at which dealers and used car sites are listing your vehicle. Make sure you are comparing the same car with similar options and mileage. If you compare incorrectly, it could cost you more time and money. For example, if you have a front-wheel drive truck and list it at the price of a four-wheel drive truck, you are going to be overpriced and you'll have trouble selling. Likewise, if you list a four-wheel drive truck at the value of a two-wheel drive truck, you will be underpriced and you'll lose money.

There are many options you can choose for selling a car, just as there are with buying a car. You need to "Just Ask" yourself what is the option that best meets your needs and talents to give you the most return on your investment. You will find that there are plenty of pros and cons to each option you consider.

Selling an Automobile by Owner

One of the most common ways to sell a vehicle is by owner. This can mean listing the car for sale on the street corner, on a lot, in the paper, online, or in multiple other ways. One of the advantages of selling the car yourself is that you can usually get more money than some of the other options I will share in this chapter. However, some of the disadvantages you will have is that you have to deal with people, and that can be a large challenge itself. You will experience people who waste your time by setting up appointments and not showing, some will ask you all types of questions and call or email you at all hours of the day only to never really be interested in the car, and, of course, you will get the low ballers.

Some other challenges that come with selling a vehicle yourself is that if something goes wrong with the car, you may have a disgruntled buyer bothering you, even if you sold the car "as is". This can become quite frightening if you had the person come to your home to purchase the car and now they know where you live. Therefore, you may want to ask yourself if you should consider setting up your meetings in front of a court-house or police station when selling a car For Sale by Owner (FSBO). It is human nature for some of these people to not give up when there is an issue with what they have purchased, and they may think it is your fault or that they were deceived by you. So be extra careful to fully disclose as much as possible about any defects with your car. I have heard horror stories about people who arrive to test drive your vehicle and leave their vehicle behind while they test drive yours and they never come back. When you call the police, you find out that the car they left was stolen and now you have no vehicle. Also, I have heard of people coming to see your car and test drive it only to say they were not interested in the car and then they come back later to steal it from you. So, be aware of some of the issues you may experience if you sell a car on your own.

Some people will come to see the car and make you an offer but want to pay with a check or at a later time. This can be a bad idea because if the check is bad and you give them the title, it is much harder to get your money, and you may end up spending a lot of time and money pursuing a person who did this. They may not even be the actual person who wrote the check, especially if the check is stolen, so you may never find them. Buyers will often want to take the car for a drive or to their mechanics to check out the car. There you risk them damaging something or other things going wrong. There are even people who will intentionally cause some type of mechanical harm to your vehicle trying to get it for a lower price.

So, you may want to make sure that you are with the potential buyer when they test drive the car, and if they want to take it to a mechanic to check it out, you can meet them there with the car. This way you can oversee what the mechanic is checking and ensure that all the issues they find are legitimate. Last but not least, you may need to go with them to a bank if they need to set up a vehicle loan for you to get paid. This means that you are losing time by having to spend your day at the bank and helping them with your car purchase. However, going to the bank with the customer ensures you get your payment if they decide to purchase the car. When selling a car on your own, "Just Ask" yourself if you can spare the time.

Clean up Your Act

Prior to selling your car, do your best to fix anything you can and to make sure your car is clean and shiny. "Just Ask" yourself what you first look at when shopping for a car. There is a lot to be said for making your car look and smell clean. People's first impressions are the look of the car, so if you have leftover fast food bags thrown on the floor and stains from eating in your car, it will be a turn off for most people, and you should not expect to get top dollar for your car, especially if it is a newer high-end vehicle. Sometimes paying a professional detail company will be money well spent if you don't have the time, tools, or knowledge to do it yourself. Professional companies have the cleaning tools and people who know how to get your car looking its best so you can sell it. To find the best detail shops, search online and look at reviews to make sure they have a reputation for doing a good job. Ask friends or contacts for recommendations. Also, you could always call some of your local car dealerships and ask them who they use for detailing their used cars. Often, they may offer a car detailing service or at least know of one you could use.

Turn off Your Lights

If you have any warning lights lit up on the dash, such as the check engine light, it is best to have the problems causing the light to turn on fixed. An inexpensive way to find out why warning lights are on is to go to a local auto parts store and have them check your engine codes for free and tell you why a specific light may be on. Also, they can provide parts to fix the issue. If it is something simple, I will generally fix it myself. If you are not sure if you can fix it yourself, you can always search YouTube and see if there are any videos showing how to fix the problem. Then you can make the decision to either fix the issue yourself or take it to a professional mechanic.

If you decide to not fix the problem, when you sell it you can at least tell prospective buyers what is wrong with the car so they can make an informed decision on whether or not to purchase your car. If you are honest and up-front with a customer, they are more apt to trust you and want to purchase from you. However, if you intentionally don't disclose something like a check engine light and they question you on it, they are going to think you either are dishonest or don't have a brain. It is always better to be honest. You may find multiple items that you can fix in your car whether mechanical or cosmetic prior to selling it. You should "Just Ask" yourself if the problem is worth fixing by comparing the cost to the value of fixing it.

For example, if you have a check engine light on for a repair that is simple to fix and the part costs twenty dollars, you will be better off fixing that item because it will make your car easier to sell. However, if your check engine light is on because the vehicle needs a new, expensive part that is not critical to operations and safety and it would cost $2,000 to fix and your car is only worth $1,000, it is not going to be worth fixing that issue, especially if your car runs fine without fixing it.

The other thing to keep in mind is how much work you want to do yourself to save you money on your vehicle. If you're mechanically inclined, it may be cheap to fix your own car prior to selling, which will get you more money and save the buyer money as well. If you can do a repair on your car for $100 that would cost $500 at a dealership and it gives you $300 more in the sale price, it would make sense to do that. Otherwise, you can expect the buyer to ask for a reduction in cost so that they can hire a mechanic to do the repair for $500.

Do You Have the Time and Talent to Sell on Your Own?
"Just Ask" yourself if you can afford the time and hassle to sell a car on your own. You will need to be patient when selling by owner if you want the best price. Having to wait to sell your car can be a problem if you have no other means of transportation and you need the money to be able to afford your next car. You can always try to get rides to work in between selling a car and buying a car, but that may get old for both parties involved if you are not able to find the right car in a reasonable amount of time.

One thing you can do is make sure you help the person giving you a ride by offering to pay for gas. Even if they don't accept money for gas, make sure that you do something nice to thank them on a weekly basis so that they know you appreciate their help and so they don't feel like they are being taken advantage of.

Selling Directly to a Dealership

Another way to sell your car is directly to a dealer or through an auction. This is a simple process, but it is generally the least profitable way to sell your car because the dealer is not going to give you top dollar for your vehicle. This is because car dealers have to take the risk that something could go wrong and they might have to fix your car. Also, if they check out your car and find something wrong before buying it, they are going to let you know about it and then adjust the purchase price accordingly. The dealer that would purchase your car outright generally wants you to trade it in so that you buy another car from them. This way the dealership can double dip by giving you a low price on your car and selling you another car for profit.

Trading in your car can have a couple of advantages. One advantage is that you don't have to deal with listing your car or with a lot of people potentially calling you wanting to see your car. When you trade your car into a dealer, there will be tax advantages, and you'll be able to drive home with a new car that day. The advantage of trading a car into a dealer is that any amount that you trade the car in for will come off what you have to pay in taxes on your next vehicle. So, if you trade a car in for $5,000 and you're buying a $10,000 vehicle, you would only pay tax on the $5,000 difference. Without a trade-in, you'll pay taxes on the full $10,000. Residents of states without sales tax don't need to worry about this.

Ask yourself if the tax savings is worth trading in your vehicle. Also, you have to ask if all the time and hassle of selling by owner is worth the difference in the price you're going to get from a dealership.

When you trade in your vehicle with a large dealership, you are more likely to get some type of warranty you won't get from a smaller dealership. Many dealerships sell aftermarket warranties on used vehicles. These warranties give the dealership a very high margin, and many times they're through a secondary market. A lot of times by just asking you can get the dealer to reduce the price of the aftermarket warranty.

Many of these warranties, even though they say they cover drive train or engine, have specific limitations, and you need to read the fine print in the warranty to understand what they truly cover. For example, if the dealership says the warranty covers engine failure but the fine print says it doesn't cover any parts that are part of standard wear, your bearings or your pistons might not be covered. That's why it is important to understand what all the details of the warranty are and to read it yourself. Don't just trust the technician or the salesperson. Because the warranty says something different, it won't stand up in court if you have a mechanical failure that is not covered because it's in writing and you signed for it.

Selling Your Car Outright to a Dealership
Some dealerships will buy a car outright from you and then resell it. Typically you're going to experience the same issues I shared with you when trading in to a dealership and getting paid less than if you sold it FSBO. However, you will then have the money in your hand to go shopping at multiple locations to find your next vehicle. It is always easier to negotiate a deal when you have cash in hand because the seller knows you are a serious buyer. Make sure you find a dealership that would directly buy your car from you and provide a written guarantee to purchase it from you within a thirty-day period so that you have time to find your next car and then sell your current car to conduct the transaction. This method gives you the flexibility to do some additional searching and shopping without feeling like you're locked into one dealership.

If you don't have additional transportation or you need a car immediately, this can be a challenge. One way to utilize this method is to search and find your vehicle first, whether it's FSBO or at another dealership, then trade your car in for cash once you have a deal secured. This will provide you the opportunity to keep using your vehicle until you find the right one to meet your needs. Keep in mind that if you use this method without cash in hand, you chance a person or dealership selling the vehicle you want to another person before you trade your other vehicle for the cash you need. Therefore, you may have to provide some type of money down to secure the deal, which can be risky if you don't know the seller. Personally, I do not give money for something that I don't receive when I purchase it, unless I know it is a legitimate company.

If you end up finding your vehicle at a dealership, you should at least compare a trade in at the dealership where you're going to purchase the car against the amount of cash you are going to get from the other dealership to sell your car outright.

No-Haggle Dealerships

If you purchased a car from a no-haggle dealership, they too will sometimes purchase the car back from you at a reasonable price. The car I purchased from CarMax that I shared about in the previous chapter was the one I ended up selling back to them a few years down the road. I had it FSBO for a very good price, but I was not getting a lot of interest in the car at that price. I had several low ball offers and a couple of more serious offers, but it ended up that CarMax paid me significantly more for my vehicle than selling it on my own, so it was a no-brainer to sell it to them. There's a lot to be said for having cash in hand when you purchase your next vehicle. If you're not comfortable dealing directly in cash, most people will take a certified cashier's check from the bank.

"Just Ask" Yourself

- Ask yourself if you can be patient enough to sell on your own.
- Ask yourself, if you were a buyer, would you buy your vehicle for sale? If not, why not?
- Ask yourself how much time you have or want to spend selling a vehicle on your own.
- Ask yourself if you have the knowledge to take the risk of buying a vehicle FSBO.
- Ask yourself if you can fix the things wrong with your vehicle and if it will bring more value to fix it than to sell it without fixing it.
- Ask yourself where a safe place would be to meet if you sell your vehicle on your own.
- Ask yourself what you can clean and shine to make your vehicle look its best and get the most money.

"Just Ask" Others

- If listing an ad in the paper, always ask for a better price than what they first offer you.
- If selling to a person yourself, always negotiate with any offer and see if you can get them to come up to a reasonable price that is acceptable for both parties.
- Ask an auto detailer for a deal to clean your car and make it look like new again.
- Ask the local dealers who they use to clean their vehicle and get them ready for sale.

- Ask local auto part shops for free testing of dash lights that may be on.
- Ask others how to fix issues with your car before selling. For example, look on blogs and YouTube for tutorials.
- If someone wants to buy your car and get a loan, ask for a deposit on the purchase of the vehicle.

"Just Ask" Savings

"I asked a buyer for $100 extra over my purchase price if they wanted me to meet them at the bank for a loan, and they paid me the extra money."

    —Kyle R., Wilmington, NC

"I asked a local dealer who they used to repair their ripped seat and I called their person. They fixed my torn seat and repainted it to look like new for $100. I am sure that it helped my car sell much faster. I would have lost several hundred dollars in the sale if it had the long six-inch tear and wear on it."

    —Sheila T., Plymouth, WI

Chapter 8
Buying a Home

In this chapter you will learn how to save money buying a home, the advantages and disadvantages of working with a realtor, how to buy For Sale by Owner, the importance of inspections, contingencies, negotiations, and sources and links for house research. Also, you will learn the benefit of understanding your own core values so you will make better choices in buying your home without worrying about keeping up with the Joneses.

Making the Largest Purchase of Your Life
Buying a home can be one of the largest purchases of your life. If you take your time and plan by asking yourself what your needs are, you will be able to make good rational decisions and hopefully save some money along the way. There are many steps in buying a home along with all the decisions that go with it. You are going to have to determine the right time to purchase your home and what will be right for your overall needs. During the next few chapters, I hope to help give you guidance so you can make good decisions along the way and come out profitable in the end. You can make money along with finding a great home that you will enjoy for years to come. I will share with you a few ways you can negotiate, find the right location, and decide whether to buy For Sale by Owner (FSBO) or use a realtor and negotiate the best interest rate for your needs.

Just Ask What Your Needs Are
One of the easiest ways to determine the right home for you is to consider what you are looking to achieve in purchasing a home. For example, are you trying to buy a larger house for your family or move closer to work? There are many reasons you might want to buy a house, but it's important that you think about it so you can focus on the right type of house, the right location, and, of course, the right budget.

Do You Need a Realtor?
Many people who buy a home work with a realtor because they do not have access to the market and they are not familiar with the process of purchasing a house and do not want to risk something going wrong with such a large purchase. Realtors can be a good

resource for buying a home, but they are out to make money. They will sell your house for any amount as long as they can get their 3% to 6% commission. And when you buy a home, they will try to get you to pay as much as possible so that they will get a higher commission. Either way, it can be a challenge to purchase a home. Most people are going to purchase a home that would take 20% to 30% of their income on a monthly basis to pay on a mortgage. Therefore, the lower the interest rate, the more likely people are to extend themselves for the "next level" up for a home.

This could be a good thing if the market takes off and they sell their home for a lot more than they paid and then buy a less expensive house in a cheaper location or just downsize and have less debt. However, most people are going to continue to buy and sell to increase their standard of living. Therefore, the more money we have, the more we want and the more we are willing to extend ourselves. If you can realize that this is a natural desire, you can train and discipline yourself to look for the best ways to make your investment profitable. Otherwise, you might regret your decision and end up living with a lot more stress in your life.

For Sale by Owner

Over the years I have bought several homes FSBO and have done well on my purchases. However, without taking the time to research the market, I could have just as easily lost money. A lot of times when a home is listed by the owner of the house, they have an emotional attachment to the home along with thinking that they can get the same amount a realtor is willing to list their house for on the market.

Realtors are out to make money and will tell you what you want to hear. A realtor knows you are speaking to several companies about listing your home with them, and they are usually going to tell you that they can get more for your house than they know the market will bear. Why is that? The realtor knows that if they can get your listing for a year, they can then sit back and wait for someone else to sell the home and still get 50% of the commission without having to do all the work associated with dealing with the clients. Of course, some realtors are very aggressive and want to sell the home themselves and keep all the commission, which is what we would all hope for.

However, the reality is that a realtor wants the listing and is more apt to tell you what you want to hear and list the house at the price you want knowing that you will never get that amount. Then, about a month after your home went on the market, they will tell you that they need to lower the price because there has been no real interest in the home yet and it must be that the price is too high. Keep in mind that the one thing realtors will tell you is that a house priced right will sell. Also, a house on the market for an extended period of time will become stale and people will lose interest in the home. When people are competing for a house, it puts the seller in a great position. The people who are competing reaffirm to the other buyer that the house price must be right because there is other interest.

This is the same with other things. When was the last time you went to buy something you thought was a great deal and it was already sold? Didn't you say to yourself, "I knew it was a great deal"?

Overpriced FSBO Homes

I often find it a little funny when a person tries to sell a house on their own and puts the price at or above the top end of the market. Then several months down the road, when the house does not sell, they hire a realtor and drop the price thousands of dollars to try to get it sold. If the price was right in the first place, it would have sold. However, sentimentality and greed sometimes get the best of people. They might have been better off listing with a realtor who knows the market, has better advertisement tools to promote the house, and has a network of people interested in real estate. If they had listed the house at 6% less than the realtor would list it for so that it is a good deal for the buyer, they most likely would have sold it on their own. Also, if the house is listed at the right price, there is always the possibility that more than one buyer could come in and make an offer and drive the price up, making you more money.

Will You Regret Having the Most Expensive Home in Your Neighborhood?

I once saw a house listed in the town where I live go on the market as a FSBO. For the first few weeks, tons of people came to view the house because it looked great and was large and beautiful. However, the people who owned the home had listed the price above the top prices for the neighborhood. It was the largest and most expensive home in the neighborhood, and the price was so high the neighbors thought the sellers were crazy.

Trying to sell the largest and most expensive house in a neighborhood can be hard, especially if you are trying to get top price in the market and the other surrounding homes don't compare. That is why you should choose the best home for your needs when you buy, otherwise, you might regret it when you try to sell your home. Regret can happen when you sell your house for less than you purchased it or when it takes a lot of time, energy, and stress to sell your home. I think most people are becoming a little wary of buying the nicest home in an average neighborhood because the markets can change and you chance losing money on your largest investment. I believe in the old saying, "Location, location, location." You need to seek out buying the smallest house in the best neighborhood and not the largest or most expensive home in an average neighborhood if you want to make the most money on your investment.

Look beyond the Overgrown Bushes and Outdated Paint

When my wife and I bought our first house, we did everything right. I guess you could say it was beginner's luck. I remember my wife telling me about the cute little house on the bulletin board at work she wanted me to take a look at. When she told me the size and that it only had a one-car garage, I laughed and asked why we would buy a house from someone listing it on a bulletin board. The house for sale scared me because it was listed FSBO. I got a realtor and started looking in the area at houses for sale in the $80,000 to $140,000 range. After a few weeks of looking, we found several nice homes, but the people selling were not very negotiable, and we found other homes that needed a lot of work.

I felt like we had really looked at the market and had a good sense of the homes in our price range. My wife came home from work and mentioned to me that she knew the people who were selling their home and they would be willing to show the home to us anytime and that they wanted to work with us. I finally gave in and decided to look at the home after work one day. I got to the home, which was located on the corner and was partially covered by two huge juniper bushes along with several overgrown shrubs that went across most of front of the house.

When we entered the 900-square-foot home, it was very nice. There was a formal dining room with built-in leaded glass hutches in the corners, a living room with original leaded glass, front bow windows, and a beautiful hand-carved fireplace mantel in the living room authentic to the era of the home. The front door was an old, original wood door with the original mailbox slot in the center and an old cast iron door knocker. The bedrooms were small and quaint with arched doors and hallways with outdated carpet on the floors and outdated paint on the walls. I lifted the corners of the carpet in the closet to check what was underneath and discovered some beautiful shining oak hardwood floors. Of course, I did not mention it to the owners, because they thought there was just a cheap subfloor beneath all the years they lived there. Also, the home was one block from the best school in town, which was going through a ten-million-dollar renovation, only two blocks from the park, and all the neighbors had large lovely homes, including a mansion right across the street with a creek running through the property.

It was a dream location. The house was priced well compared to what we had seen. Next was the negotiation of the price, which I will discuss further in my negotiation section. The people were asking over $100,000, and we offered them $90,000, which they accepted. We then enjoyed the home for a couple of years and decided to move with my company for a great job opportunity. At that time, my company had a relocation package, which included the sale of my home and the payment of 6% to a realty company. I negotiated with my company and asked them if they would pay me 3% if I sold the house on my own. They agreed. I then listed the home as FSBO for $118,000. Two days later, the house was sold. I not only got the $118,000 but I also received a 3% bonus on the sale for a total amount of $121,540 dollars of which $51,540 dollars was equity when we sold. What a deal! We were very pleased. It was a great return on our initial investment of $20,000 down on the $90,000 house two years earlier.

Again, to review the numbers, we purchased the home for $90,000 but paid $20,000 down, so we owed on a $70,000 mortgage. Over the two-year period we lived there, we put in about $5,000 in repairs and got a total return of about $46,540, which was a lot of money. These numbers do not include the equity we built up by paying our mortgage payments along with our tax deductions on the interest, which was another $3,000 gain on our end. Also, the company paid all our closing and moving costs, so we only gained in taking the promotion and moving.

Should You Continue Buying FSBO?

After selling our home in Walla Walla, Washington, and making a great profit, we moved to North Carolina with my company. When we moved, we bought another great home in a gated community. The owners were about to list their home with a realtor and told me they would sell the house for less if they did not use a realtor. I knew right there that their price would save me 6%. Also, the person selling the home happened to be my boss and was moving back to Walla Walla, Washington, and could try to negotiate the same deal with the company I did and get 3% more in selling FSBO instead of listing with a realtor.

We found out their asking price, and my kind wife started looking at comparable homes in the area. She spent the next several days looking at homes to try and determine if the home we wanted to buy from my boss was a better deal than other homes on the market listed by a realtor. Again, I did not want to buy an overpriced home from a person who had too much sentimental value built into their asking price. After looking for several days, she was able to determine that their asking price was fair. In fact, the realtor we were using mentioned she was aware of a FSBO home she may be listing and that we would love the home. My wife told her that we had already looked at the home with the owner and that we would work directly with the seller if we went in that direction. The realtor was then open and honest with us and told us we would not find a better deal for that price in that neighborhood. So, we purchased the home.

We lived in that house for a couple of years and moved again with my company, and we were able to sell the home for a very nice profit that was tax-free because we had lived there for two years. Check the tax laws when buying or selling a home to see if there is any benefit for you and how you should structure your purchase. Because we had lived in our house for two years, we were able to sell the home with no tax implications of the profit that we would make off it, and were able to put the money into our next home as the down payment. A lot of times you can find this tax information out for free online. It's very simple to do and is well worth your time.

Get a Home Inspection

Having a home inspection done by a professional is money well spent if you don't have a lot of knowledge of what to look for as far as house defects. A home inspection will assure that your heating, plumbing, roofing, basement, and electrical are up to code and that you are aware of any major issues before you buy your new home.

There is no guarantee the inspector will find everything wrong with the home, but when they do find things, you will be thankful that you are aware of any problems before you make the biggest investment of your life. Just Ask yourself if you would like to buy a home in the winter and find out in the spring that the basement floods. A home inspector can see critical things, such as roofing problems, cracked foundations, and incorrect electrical connects. Once you have an inspection report, you can use it to your advantage when finalizing your purchase and can request that the seller fix any issues prior to closing.

If you ask the seller to fix everything on the list, they may not want to and then you will have to decide what to do. Many times you can negotiate the large things or a credit at closing so that you can make the repairs yourself. For example, if the roof is in need of replacement and it would cost $10,000 to repair, you could request that they repair the roof or that they give you a credit at closing for the amount. If you are handy, you may request cash back at closing and then do the repairs yourself. This way you will save more money and put the extra cash back in your pocket.

Most sellers expect to negotiate when selling a home. The important thing is to ask for the problems to be fixed when you find them. If they are not willing to fix them, ask what they are willing to do, and you will most likely get some type of repair or reduction in price. Don't walk away from a deal without negotiating unless there is something critically wrong that you can't reasonably repair. There have been times where I ask for something, and they come back with an amount that is not acceptable, but as I kept negotiating, we met in the middle and both parties benefited. Keep in mind that no seller wants to lose an opportunity of selling their home because it could take a long time for another buyer to make the next offer. So, always listen to all offers and negotiate.

Just Ask for More Than You Need When Negotiating
In many ways, buying a home is like buying a car. It is easy to negotiate some simple things that will bring value and add money to your pocket. You can ask the seller to provide a home warranty that will generally cover mechanical failures

of key items like furnaces, ovens, stoves, and other items. You will need to review the home warranty policy prior to accepting the offer to make sure it covers what you need. Many times a seller, for a small amount, can purchase a home warranty so that if anything major goes wrong with the home—from your air conditioning and heating to your refrigerator and stove—it will be repaired. Typically the time period for this insurance is a year, but it could be longer.

A lot of times you can get what's called a curtain allowance or carpet allowance. Many times the owners don't want to put more money into the house only to have a prospective buyer say they don't like the carpet color or the window shades or the paint or something like that, so they'll offer a set amount of money toward a carpet allowance or some other type of allowance that would give the buyer money back toward replacing those.

Have a List Prepared before Buying a Home
If you're going to finance a home, always do your research up front to ensure you have preapproved credit before looking to purchase. In general, a bank will give you a letter stating you're prequalified for a certain purchase value. The bank first does a background check and credit check and runs you through a general process to ascertain that you can afford the home you're looking to purchase.

So, for example, if you want to purchase a home in a price range between $50,000 and $200,000, the bank can give you a prequalification letter stating you're approved for up to $200,000. When you're negotiating to buy a home, realtors use your preapproval letter as leverage when negotiating the deal to communicate to the seller that you have the money available to purchase the home. Sellers of the home generally prefer to sell their home to buyers who are preapproved and have no contingencies on the sale. A contingency is something that a potential buyer might put on the offer to purchase their home. A typical contingency is based on the ability to secure a mortgage through a financial institution. Another contingency could be the ability to sell their house before they finalize the purchase of your home. A lot of sellers don't like a contingent offer, especially when it depends on the sale of another person's home before they can buy. Therefore, if you're a buyer and you can come in and make an offer as a preapproved, prequalified buyer with no contingencies, a seller is more likely to take your offer, even if it's lower than the other offer from the person with the contingency. They know you can close the deal quickly, and they get their cash in hand and move on.

The other thing you can do is negotiate with the realtor who is either selling the home or supporting you as the purchaser of the home. Realtors work on commission. If you are a buyer, you can often negotiate with the realtor or realtors if you're close to making a deal for them to make a concession in their commission rate to make the deal go through. A lot of times the realtor will give up part of their commission, which goes to the buyer or seller, to help close the deal so they can get their money and move on to their next sale. So, for example, if you're purchasing a house that is priced at $100,000, and you really want to buy it for $98,000, go back to the realtors and say, "You know, I really want to buy the house, but I needed it to be at $98,000." Then "Just Ask" the realtors if they would be willing to split that $2,000 cost among themselves to close the deal. In essence, each realtor gives up 1% of their commission, so instead of getting 3% each, they would get 2% each. Realtors often do this to close a deal.

Just Ask for a Better Interest Rate

When you get your initial approval letter from the bank, you'll generally know what type of interest rate you qualify for. Just like when you're car shopping, it's important to shop around for the best rate when you're looking to buy a home. Many times mortgage companies will tell you that if the interest rates drop within the thirty-day window before you close, they will lower your rate, but it must drop at least a quarter percent before they will drop the price. However, in all my days of buying homes, I have never had them do that for me yet. I have been able to negotiate a better interest rate prior to fully locking in the rate by following the market and seeing the rates go up and down and then calling the bank to lock in the rate when I see it drop. What I mean by locking in your rate is you have to actually tell the bank you're ready to lock in an interest rate that's available, and then that rate will only be held for a short period of time, usually around thirty days, so that you have time to close on your home. You're not generally able to lock in a rate if you don't have the amount you need to borrow nor the house identified because it may take you more than several months to get the deal finalized.

Prior to locking in your interest rate, check with other banks to ensure you got the best deal, even though you may only be working with one brokerage or mortgage broker. I have been able to go back to the financial institution or mortgage company prior to locking in my interest rate and negotiate them down an eighth of a point, which actually is a lot of money if you look at it over a fifteen- or thirty-year mortgage. Another tip when dealing with the mortgage broker is to understand all the fees and costs they charge for the closing of your home. Some of the fees are standard, but some of their fees can sometimes be negotiated.

Paying Cash for a Home Can Save You

If you are fortunate enough to have cash to pay for a house outright, consider doing it. Many times you can negotiate a reduced rate with a bank for a foreclosed house. Banks really like it when people have the cash up front to make a quick purchase rather than having to set up a mortgage. Real estate assets cost banks money, so they want to sell quickly.

Many people hear about all the stories of buying foreclosures and bank-owned properties and tax-sale properties, but they're not always easy to buy and they're not always a great deal. You have to do the same type of work and due diligence as you would if buying a house FSBO or from a realtor. Many times the houses for sale from the bank or from the state or city can be in poor shape because the people who lived there defaulted on their mortgage or taxes and let the place deteriorate or maybe their health is in poor shape or someone passed away. Whatever the situation is, a lot of times, houses like that may need work. You will have to evaluate if you want to take on the project and if there is enough room for all the time and repairs you may need to make it worth your while. If you make a combined income of $50,000 a year and you can put in two years of work on a home and get a $50,000 increase in value, it's like getting a 50% increase in your pay.

Also, if you live in the house for two years, with the current tax laws, you would not have to pay any taxes on the gain if you sold the house. I've seen houses that were repossessed by the bank that were beautiful on the exterior. When I went inside, the previous owners had stolen all the chandeliers or put holes in the walls or left the water on so that it ran down through the ceiling. They do this just to be mean because they're getting their house taken away, and there's a lot of emotion tied to that. Be very careful and do your research.

The other thing with buying a repossessed home or bank foreclosure is that it could take many months before the bank gets back to you regarding if they're even willing to look at or accept your offer. I've had offers in to multiple banks before for different houses and never even got a response to tell me if they are interested in my offer or not. You have to be patient and know that it can take some time for the banks to respond.

Should You Finance?

When you finance a home, it is better to take out a low rate mortgage if you can invest your money in something that brings you a good rate of return on your investment. So, if you can get an interest rate for 4% and then invest the rest of your money to make 7%, it makes more sense to invest to make the higher interest rate on your money. Keep in mind that you may get to write off the interest paid on your home mortgage, so you have to consider that when choosing whether or not to finance. Also, you have to ask if you are okay being in debt, especially if you can afford to pay it off. Sometimes, there is peace of mind knowing that you have no debt. However, if your debt is making you more money, then you will have to train yourself to understand that you are using your financial savvy to your benefit and that it is a good thing. Just be careful not to get overleveraged by your debts.

Can You Afford to Lose Your Home?

When you purchase a home, it is important to plan ahead so that if you have a financial problem, you can survive in today's economy. If you are married, I am recommending that you purchase a home based on the income of the lowest income provider in your family. This way, should one person lose their job, you can still afford the mortgage payments and won't be put in a precarious situation. Also, you can invest the other partner's money in order to build more financial security and get you closer to retiring debt free. A good rule of thumb is to not spend more than 25% of your annual income on a home, even though the banks may lend you upwards of 30% based on your income. "Just Ask" yourself if you want to take the risk of losing your biggest asset because of a job loss or, God forbid, an illness. If you put $20,000 down to finance a $100,000 house and default on your loan, you will lose the equity of the $20,000 you put down on the home. Also, you will get bad credit and may not ever be able to afford a home again. If you plan ahead, you can easily avoid this situation.

"Just Ask" Yourself

- Ask yourself what the best neighborhood is to buy your home from a resale value standpoint.
- Ask yourself if you are buying your home as a status symbol or if you are treating it as an investment you can enjoy while you live there.
- Ask yourself if you really need to "Keep up with the Joneses" to find self-value.
- Ask yourself what type and size of home you really need to be happy.
- Ask yourself what you could do with the extra money you would have if you bought a reasonably priced home that you can pay off.
- Ask yourself if you could meet your financial goals sooner if you buy a more modestly priced home.
- Ask yourself if you can get by if you or your partner lose your job.

"Just Ask" Others

- Ask the realtors to reduce their commission to make the deal go through.
- Ask for better interest rates with the bank when shopping around for a lender.
- Ask for a better deal if you can afford to pay cash for a home.
- Ask the seller for a home warranty.
- Ask for the items found during the home inspection to be corrected or at least for a money credit to be made at closing.
- If you are ever in a position where you can't pay your loan, ask your lender for help with a better payment schedule until you can get back on your feet.
- Ask the mortgage company if they can waive any special fees they have or if they have any specials if you sign up for things like auto pay, direct checking, etc.
- Ask your mortgage provider if you can make early payments on the home without penalty.
- Ask your accountant or tax advisor if they can provide free advice on the best tax savings strategy when buying a home.

"Just Ask" Savings

"I asked a realtor to represent me when buying a For Sale by Owner home. They helped me negotiate a price and did all the contractual work so I was protected and only charged the seller

2%. I ended up getting a great deal and had an instant equity of $15,000."

—Jamie L., Chicago, IL

"I asked my mortgage provider if I could get an extra .25% off my mortgage rate to match their competition, and they beat the other mortgage company by 1/8 percent. This saved me thousands of dollars over the life of my mortgage."

—John H., Ann Arbor, MI

"I asked for $20,000 in repair costs on a home that I was buying 'as is,' even though I knew I was going to still buy it to renovate. I was still able to negotiate $2,000 from the seller."

—Chris H., Stevens Point, WI

"I had an offer on my home that was lower than I wanted to accept. The realtors both gave up 1% of the rates they charged. So I got 2% off their 6% commission rate, which saved me $5,000 on the sale of my $250,000 house. I got $5,000 more in my sale."

—Dave M., Menomonee, MI

Chapter 9
Selling a Home

If you are going to sell the largest purchase of your life, you are most likely going to want to get the maximum profit in your sale. To do this, you are going to have to "Just Ask" yourself a lot of questions and prepare to take your heart and emotions out of your sale, unless you want your emotions to get in the way of maximizing your profit. Many people get very emotional when preparing to sell a home that they worked so hard to buy and put a lot of time and money into. Many people, including realtors and buyers, may have opinions on what you need to do to get the most money for your home. This is why it is important that you come up with a list of things that "everyone" is asking you to do so that you can review them yourself and decide what is realistic for your situation and what you are willing to trade for the time and money it takes to sell your home. I will be covering some of the basic things you can do to maximize your profit. Just keep in mind that you have to decide what is best for you. For some, the extra money is not worth the stress, and for others, it may be. Either way I will provide you information so you can decide what you want to do and not let others guide you down the wrong path.

Do You Need a Realtor?
When making a decision to sell your home, you have to decide if you will use a realtor or sell it on your own. Most people will use a realtor because it takes a lot of the fright out of having to deal with showing your home, listing your home, and dealing with legal matters. If you don't like to deal with people and set up showings of your home, using a realtor might be a good option for you.

Without a realtor, you will need to do the following on your own: research the best listing price for your home, set up the listing, promote it, show your home to prospective buyers, and set up a purchase agreement. If you don't have the time to do all of that, you will need a realtor. Selling a home without a realtor is not simply placing a For Sale sign in the yard.

As you will see, there is a lot to selling a home on your own and it can make you more money, but if you're not experienced or don't follow my techniques, you could lose a lot of money in your sale. Ask yourself if you can afford the risk. Also, speak to others who have sold For Sale by Owner (FSBO) or who are familiar with what it takes to be successful so you can make good decisions. A realtor can cost you some money, but they are very knowledgeable about the markets and can help you in many areas.

One of the real advantages to using a realtor is that they can list your home on the Multiple Listing Service (MLS), which is a suite of services real estate brokers use to list their properties and share other information between realtors. By having a realtor who has access to the MLS, your listing will reach millions of people. People who are not licensed realtors or brokers do not have access to the MLS, except through the service provided by your realtor or searching the internet to find listed homes on sites like Realtor.com, Redfin.com, Trulia.com, and others that tie into the MLS. You can find homes listed on these sites, but you cannot list your home for sale on these sites because they are tied in the MLS. According to Realtor.com, only 8% of homes in 2017 were sold FSBO, and the price of the homes sold by the owners were $39,000 less on average than those sold using the MLS system. Therefore, based on the data, most people should and will use a realtor. However, keep in mind that you will pay anywhere from 3% to 6% on average to use a realtor, so their service is not free. But if you make more money with a realtor than the commission costs, it is well worth it.

Cost of Using a Realtor

The realtor fee is only part of the cost for a realtor. Just because they ask for a 6% commission does not mean you can't "Just Ask" for a reduced rate. Many times, most realtors will negotiate a smaller commission fee if it will help the deal go through for the buyer and seller. However, this means less money in their pocket, so depending on the housing market, this could be a challenge. As I shared previously, if you don't provide a fair rate of commission, you could be missing out on other realtors showing your house. If the list realtor does not sell your home, they have to split the commission with the realtor who brings the buyer. For example, if you list a $100,000 home at 6% commission, and the listing realtor sells the home, they get the full 6% or $6,000 for selling your home. If you have another realtor come in who is not the listing broker and they sell the home, they and the listing broker each get 3% commission, which is still only 6% out of your pocket. However, they each only get $3,000, and that money most likely needs to go to their real estate company, so they only get a small percentage of the amount.

Now, if you talk your realtor into only getting 4% commission, you may turn off other realtors wanting to show your home. What incentive does the other realtor have to sell your home if they are only going to get 2% if they find the buyer? If they have a potential buyer who is willing to buy a $100,000 home, do you think they would rather have them buy from a realtor who has a higher commission when they get 1% or 2% more? It makes sense to match the market rate and not get too greedy. When you have an offer on the table, you then have a little more negotiation power. I have "Just Asked" each realtor to come down a little on their commission to get a sale to work for all parties. Especially when I get a real low offer from a buyer and the realtor may lose the sale. It gives all parties incentive to move a little.

Always Negotiate
Don't ever walk away from an offer without trying to negotiate a sale. Early in my real estate buying, I had a fair offer on the table from a buyer a short time after listing my home, and the realtor convinced me to ignore the offer when I wanted to negotiate. The realtor felt we could get more money, and the house was fresh on the market. It ended up that when I sold the home over a month later, I got less than my first offer along with carrying additional costs I paid.

"Just Ask" If You Can Sell the Home Yourself
As I shared with you, I have done well selling by owner. If you are going to be successful in selling and buying FSBO, you will have to be patient, diligent, and disciplined. You'll have to invest time to come out ahead. This chapter provides an overview of what it takes to sell successfully, and there is much more to selling on your own than I can cover in a short chapter.

Just Ask for a Free Appraisal
If you are going to sell FSBO, you must do your research and find your home's value. You can determine the value in several ways, but you must be sure you know it because you can lose much of your potential profit if you are wrong. A good time to determine the price is when choosing a realtor. Typically, a

realtor will give you a free market comparison on the price at which they feel you could list your home to sell quickly in the current market. It is recommended if you are going to have a housing market comparison that you meet with multiple realtors from different companies prior to making your decision on whether or not to use a realtor. If you decide to use FSBO, you will have the needed market comparisons to price your home competitively. You could hire an appraiser as well so that you can get a good feel of the value of your home, but you would be foolish if you did this and did not at least compare the results to that which a realtor can provide you for free.

One other way, but it is not recommended as a standalone review, is to research homes for sale in your area. Keep in mind that a simple review is generally not enough because you may not know enough about the location, details, and upgrades of those homes. For example, you may see what looks like the exact same home as yours online, but there could be factors that would make it significantly more or less valuable than your home. A realtor is generally more knowledgeable about other homes for sale in the area and can help save you a lot of money in mistakes if you "Just Ask" them questions. Imagine if you see a home that looks the same as yours and you price it the same and you sell right away only to find out that you could have made $50,000 more on the sale of your home. The other home may have backed up to a busy highway or was in a less desirable neighborhood and you did not realize it. Be careful and get a good comparison. Once you have all this information, you can then determine the price at which to list your home.

Do You Have Curb Appeal?

There have been several times when I have seen people pull up to a house for sale and not even go into the home because of the outward appearance of the home. People need to feel the house is inviting. A few ways you can do this is by cleaning and organizing your yard. This may include mowing and edging the lawn, updating the landscaping and shrubbery, painting the front door or home if needed. These are just a few examples, but it is amazing how a fresh cut lawn with nice crisp edging and a swept sidewalk can invite a guest into your home.

If you don't have a talent for seeing these types of things, you can ask a realtor or landscaping company for their advice. Just be careful that you don't get carried away and spend more money in updates than it is worth. If a realtor tells you that painting the outside of your home will get you an additional $10,000, and it will only cost you $5,000 to paint, it makes perfect sense to invest the money. However, if you are told that you should put in underground sprinklers and all new landscaping for a cost of $10,000 and you will only get an additional $5,000 in the sale, it may not be worth it, unless you must have these options to compete with other homes in order to sell your house. You must train yourself to "Just Ask" if the time, money, and effort are worth the return. Again, you only have so much time to live and give, and money potential is unlimited. Choose wisely so you don't look back years later and wonder where all your time went.

Are You Ready to Clean up Your Act?
Just like your parents said, go clean your room! You will need to clean your home if you are going to get top dollar. Cleaning your home does not mean that you just vacuum the floors. You need to prepare by decluttering, depersonalizing, and cleaning. Also, you need to mentally prepare yourself to make these changes without being offended. One of the first steps is to put together a pre-selling/staging checklist. If you go to my website, JustAskTheBook.com, you will find a pre-sale checklist that you can print out and use when getting ready to sell your home. The list should have things on it like: fix the hole in the wall from when little Jimmy got mad at Suzie; repaint the hallway from all the little kiddies' handprints; replace the shag lime green carpet from the 1950s; and any other defect from a potential buyer's perspective.

If some of the items you find that need fixing are beyond your skill level, you will need to hire a professional to help you. Sellers are sometimes afraid to make the needed changes to maximize the value of their home, especially when it comes to removing personal pictures on the wall or special mementos that have a lot of meaning to them. Realtors are correct when they say to set your home up for showings. Prior to selling a home, I make sure all the rooms have everything fixed and painted in a neutral color along with removing any wall hangings people might find distasteful. Also, I make sure the flooring is updated or in very good shape. A big turn-off for buyers is rooms being painted in a color they don't like. Often people cannot see beyond the paint on the wall. You have to paint the walls so that they can see envision how their things would fit in the home.

Part of this process will need to be decluttering your home as well. Many times, less is more, especially when it comes to selling your house. If you have smaller furniture, it will make the home look larger. This may mean taking out the leaf in your dining room table and removing a couple of chairs. It may also mean removing extra furniture and belongings to make your house more presentable. I have removed most of my furniture and cleaned out all the closets in the past prior to listing my home. People don't want to see your belongings, and when you overcrowd a room, they cannot envision how their furniture will fit. If you have the room empty, they can walk the area and try to determine where their belongings will fit.

However, the best way to really organize your home is to "stage" it. This means to make it look like a showplace when people come in. You can do this with your own belongings, or you can rent furniture and stage it that way. There are also companies you can pay to stage it. I have staged homes many times for selling by moving out all my belongings to my new home and then renting furniture to stage the home for sale. In the same way that some people cannot see beyond the paint, sometimes people cannot see how their belongings will fit in an empty home. So you have to find a happy middle ground, and each home will be different, so don't be afraid to "Just Ask" others for their opinion. In order to stage a home, you may have to sell or donate your belongings so that you have the needed room to make your house look the best it can. Just don't be afraid of change, because this is a tool that can bring in more money when you sell your home.

Are Animals Attacking Your Potential Sales?

Many people have animals, but it is always a turn-off for a potential buyer to see, hear, or smell animals in the house during a showing. Buyers may have their own pets, but they don't want to see signs of your pets in the home. For example, scratched carpet, scratched or stained floors, clawed doors, litter boxes, off odors, and so forth. The best thing you can do if you have pets is to make sure you do not have them, or any signs of them, in the home during a showing. This means, putting away or removing litter boxes from sight if you have cats, removing feeding dishes, beds, animal toys, cages, and so forth.

This may be a lot of work, but it will help you sell your home faster than if you kept them in there. If you have off odors from pets, it is best to have your home professionally cleaned to make it the most presentable possible. You just have to decide if a little extra effort is worth the possible extra time and money you can gain by being prepared. Keep in mind that if you are selling at time when there is a lot of competition on the market, these things become more critical. If there are no homes listed for sale in your area or if people are outbidding each other to purchase in your area, these things may not be as critical when it comes to selling. However, the more competitive the market, the more you need to do to have your home stand out in a good way from the others.

Are You Willing to be Priced Out of the Market?

It does not matter if you place your home with a realtor for sale or sell it on your own, be careful to price it right or your home will be stuck on the market for a long time and will get stale and may not sell. When using a realtor, you will need to determine the best realtor to meet your needs. This means you will have to interview several of them to determine the best fit for your needs. You should speak to other people who have used the realtors you are reviewing and get their opinions on what they liked and did not like about their service.

Also, you have to be careful not to let the price at which the realtor tells you they will list your house influence your decision. Many times a realtor will tell you they can get you more money than the other realtors, and then when you sign a contract with them to list your property for six months to a year, things can change. (See "For Sale by Owner" in Chapter 8).

What Are the Carrying Costs If You Don't Sell?

You have to look at all your costs to carry the home while it is listed on the market, especially if you are not living there and you are paying another mortgage at the same time. These monies can add up quickly if you are not careful. Look at your monthly mortgage, tax, utility, and insurance costs. These can add up to thousands of dollars per month if you are not careful. Add up your carrying costs so that you are well aware of your expenses. This will help you when negotiating as well. For example, if you have an offer on your home after your home has been on the market for six months and there have been no other offers, you need to consider all your costs. If the offer comes in $3,000 below your asking price and your carrying costs are $1,500/per month, you should negotiate the price within reason, trying not to lose the potential buyer.

If it takes another six months for your next offer, you will be out an additional $9,000 out of pocket, along with the stress of paying two properties and any other stress associated with the sale. Take a few minutes and go to my website and use my Free Carrying Cost Calculator so that you can have the tools to make a better decision.

Don't Regret the Sale

No matter at what price you end up selling your home or how long it takes, be content with your final price when it sells. It is human nature for us to second guess whether we should have asked for more money. If you plan ahead and trust all your research and your home sells right away, it is a good thing. Just be thankful and move on and be content. If your home does not sell fast and you end up taking less money to get it sold, be content and feel blessed that you sold your home, especially if you did not lose money. You cannot always get top dollar for everything you sell, and there is more to life than money. As long as you are able to keep moving ahead, know that selling your house was a good thing.

Don't Allow Your Home to Be Foreclosed

I have known people who have lived in a home for many years and have built up some good equity or even paid off the mortgage on the home. Then, some type of tragedy occurs and they end up losing their home. When I grew up, my neighbor lost his job and could not work due to an injury to his eye and arm. He did not owe anything on his home except for state taxes, but he was not paying them. He owed $10,000 in taxes and lost a property valued at $90,000. The reason this occurred is because he did not fight back. I don't mean physically fight, but mentally he was worn out and did not think through his options. He just sat there as the foreclosure loomed overhead like an ominous thunderstorm. He could have sold the home for $80,000–90,000, paid the taxes, and bought a less expensive home and still survived.

Instead, he let the walls fall in around him until a realtor came and "helped him out" by paying off the taxes and giving him a few thousand dollars in his pocket and then evicting him from the home. The realtor purchased the home for less than $15,000 and sold it for tens of thousands more. The homeowner got very little and was still evicted. It was a real tragedy that emotionally impacted me greatly because I was not able to help him at the time.

Sometimes we allow our situation to overwhelm us and then get depressed and let a tragedy occur that could have been prevented. I want to encourage you to fight back if you are ever in a situation like this. You can reach out to many other people and nonprofit agencies that may be able to provide you with courage and support. "Just Ask" for help when you need it. Don't let the walls fall down around you without seeking help. As I have shared in other sections of this book, most people want to help you. You just need to ask. Please see the blog section on my website for other people's examples of what they have experienced, how they got help, and how they were encouraged. If you use my principle of "Just Asking," you will get help.

"Just Ask" Yourself

- Ask yourself if your house is ready and in show condition to sell your home for the most value.
- Ask yourself what the bottom line you are willing to sell your home is so that you are prepared mentally to negotiate as offers come in.
- Ask yourself which realtor is going to represent your needs the best. Don't just go by a friend's recommendation without doing your own research.
- Ask yourself how you will feel internally if your home sells in only a few days or how you will feel if you don't sell for a long time.
- Ask yourself if trying to get top dollar means you are chancing having your home on the market for longer and making more mortgage payments that could eat up the extra money you're trying to gain.
- If you are facing foreclose, ask yourself if you are better off selling and get some equity or sitting and waiting to be evicted.
- Ask yourself if you are really organized enough and in a market where you could sell on your own or if you should use a realtor who has exposure to many more people in the market.

"Just Ask" Others

- Ask multiple realtors for an assessment of your home's values and what they will do to get your home sold.

- Ask your realtor for help staging your home.
- Ask your realtor for help in fixing up your home and contacts for doing the repairs in a cost-effective manner if you don't have the time or talent to do it yourself.
- Ask the realtor for a commission break if they sell the home themselves.
- Ask the bank or state what they can do to help you out if you work with them and you are in a position of foreclosure.
- Ask local cleaning services to help you prepare for your showing.
- Ask friends or family members if they can watch your pets for a short period while your home is for sale.
- Ask the realtor to bring cold water and cookies for each showing to help prospective buyers feel welcome and have a good memory of your home.
- If it makes the deal go through, ask realtors to take a small percentage concession if your home offer is lower than you can afford to take.

"Just Ask" Savings

"I asked a realtor how much my home was worth and had an agreement with them that if I brought the buyer, I would pay them nothing. I listed my home and sold it myself FSBO for $5,000 more than they told me it was worth and saved 6% commission for another $12,000. I saved a total of $17,000."
    —John Z., Seattle, WA

"I asked a friend to stay at her place when listing my home because I was not organized and was too busy working. My home was staged for free by the realtor and sold in one month for close to my asking price. All I did was speak to a friend and the realtor."
    —Jenny O., Bedford, IL

"I asked my realtor for contacts to repair several items in my home and repaint it a neutral color. I had all my items fixed by their contact and it saved me over $1,000 compared to my other quotes because I received the realtor's reduced rate. I not only saved money but I also sold my home."
    —Patrick K., Tacoma, WA

"I asked the bank for a reduced mortgage payment when I was under hardship and thought I was going to lose my home to foreclosure. They reviewed my current finances and lowered my payment in half while I was getting back on my feet. I was able to make my mortgage payments, keep my credit good, and save my family home."

—Sal M., Stevens Point, WI

"I had my home under foreclosure. I allowed a buyer to purchase the home directly from the bank before it was sold at auction. In return, I got an apartment paid for a year and some money to help me out versus being evicted with nothing."

—Ruth T., Linwood, WI

"I asked the realtor to help me get my home ready for staging because all my furniture was outdated. They had a company come in and stage my home professionally and my home sold in two days, and they covered the cost out of their commission. I know it would have taken a lot longer to sell my home with all the clutter."

—Justin P., Elk Hart, WI

Chapter 10
Is the Cost of College Worth It?

In this chapter you will learn how much more money you can earn in your lifetime for each level of education you achieve. You will learn techniques for saving money on your education, including buying your books, being able to negotiate the cost of your college, and applying for financial aid and scholarships.

Increase Your Earning Potential with a College Degree
Are you asking yourself if getting a college degree is worth it? If you are, you're not alone. Many people question if the cost and time of a college degree is worth it. The answer, in short, is yes. It is worth it for many people because a degree will help them get the job they want. There are many specialty careers that require specific training and/or a degree to work in a certain field. So, if you have a desire to work in a field that requires a degree, you will need a college education. The good news is that you'll be working in a field that you have chosen as a career and you will benefit financially.

Education Cost
The average cost of college has risen to $46,950 per year for a private institution and about $20,770 per year for in-state tuition rates at a state-run college as of 2018, according to College Raptor's online information. So, to obtain a bachelor's degree in four years you would have an education valued at $187,800 for a private college and $83,080 for a public college at in-state tuition rates. Many times people will say that you need a degree to get a job. More often, what they are trying to say is that if you want a higher paying job, you will need a college degree.

According to the US Bureau of Labor Statistics, a person with a high school education will earn about $1.4 million on average over a forty-year work span, and a person with a bachelor's degree would earn about $2.4 million over the same time frame. So, if you would like to make a million more dollars than the average non-degreed person, go to school. "Just Ask" yourself how much quicker you could become a millionaire if you make an extra million in your lifetime. Just think, you can take the extra million made over your working career to make even more money so it can benefit you along with giving you more freedom to help others.

Used Books May Be Your Answer

Many times you can get a great deal if you buy your textbooks used rather than new. There are many ways you can do this. It may be as simple as asking the college bookstore if they sell used textbooks, speaking to the professor of the class to see if they know of any people who have a used textbook for sale, or even looking online for used book trades. If you go to my website, JustAskTheBook.com, you will find a link to book traders.

Discounts for College?

When you apply for college, you should always try for scholarships and any financial aid they are willing to provide. However, even if you don't get a lot of money for scholarships, you can "Just Ask" the college financial aid department if they can give you a grant to cover expenses that scholarships don't cover. I know someone who did this successfully. However, you need to ask and pursue these opportunities or you will not save as much as you can. Again, my goal is not only for you to "Just Ask" yourself whether you need something but also to "Just Ask" others for help as well. There is nothing wrong with asking in a nice way because most people like to help when possible.

Lifetime Earnings

The following charts show how much money you can earn over your lifetime based on your education level.

Educational Attainment	Unemployment Rate (%)	Meian Weekly Earnings ($)	Median Yearly Earnings ($) (based on 52 weekly year)	Median Lifetime Earnings ($) (based on 40 years of employment)
Doctoral Degree	1.5	$1,743.00	$ 90,636.00	$ 3,625,440.00
Professional Degree	1.5	$1,836.00	$ 95,472.00	$ 3,818,880.00
Master's Degree	2.2	$1,401.00	$ 72,852.00	$ 2,914,080.00
Bachelor's Degree	2.5	$1,173.00	$ 60,996.00	$ 2,439,840.00
Associate's Degree	3.4	$ 836.00	$ 43,472.00	$ 1,738,880.00
Some College, No Degree	4	$ 774.00	$ 40,248.00	$ 1,609,920.00
High School Diploma	4.6	$ 712.00	$ 37,024.00	$ 1,480,960.00
Less Than High School Diploma	6.5	$ 520.00	$ 27,040.00	$ 1,081,600.00
Source: Bureau of Labor and Statatics 2018				

Median Yearly Earnings ($)
(based on 52 week year)

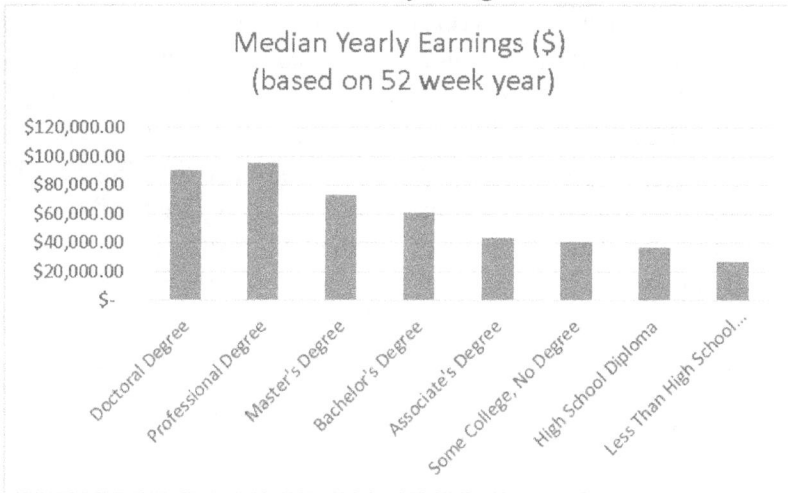

Median Lifetime Earnings ($)
(based on 40 years of employment)

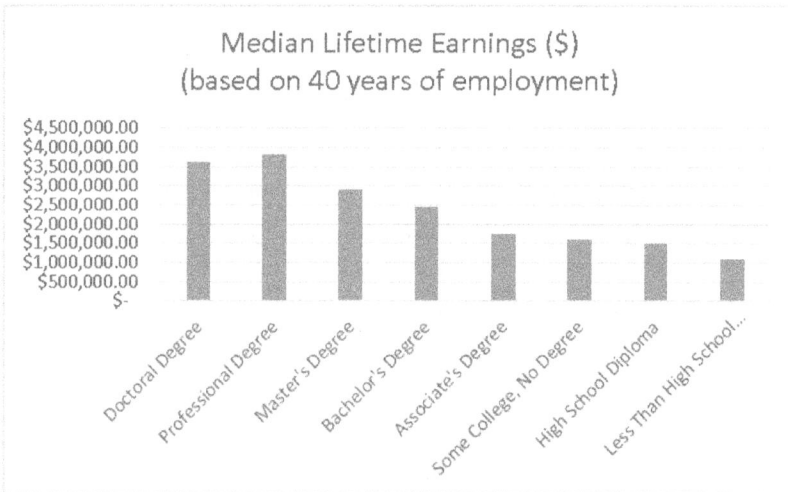

Financial Aid

No matter how much money you have, you should always apply for financial aid when you look at attending college or other technical training for which you have to pay out-of-pocket expenses. Financial aid comes from many sources, such as grants, private loans, Federal Student Loans, scholarships, and other types of loans. Financial aid is available from many sources, such as governmental agencies, colleges, and sometimes private foundations. In order to apply for Federal Aid, a person must first fill out a free application. If you go to my website, JustAskTheBook.com, you will find a link to many of the forms I mention in this book. The Free Application for Federal Student Aid (FAFSA) is just one of many forms I provide for your benefit.

Many private universities will require you to fill out applications for financial aid, such as the College Scholarship Service Profile (CSS Profile), which is an application distributed by the college boards that allows college students to apply for financial aid. Most public institutions do not use the CSS Profile to make decisions about whether a student is eligible for financial aid. Unlike the FAFSA application, the CSS Profile has a fee that can change yearly. Typically, the cost is about twenty-five dollars for submission of the CSS to the first college and an additional fee per additional college where the application will be sent.

What Are Grants?
Grants are typically a needs- and merit-based form of free money for you to use toward your educational expenses. Grants typically do not require any payback and usually are based on the financial needs for the student depending on the expected amount that a family (parents or others) will be expected to pay toward their educational expenses. Also, grants are determined by academic merit, such as a student's grade point average (GPA), and other academic merits you have received in your pre-college schooling. Many of these benefits will extend to post-college education as well. So take the time to "Just Ask" the educational institution you plan on attending how you can get the most financial benefit for your schooling.

Don't Be Loaner, Rather Be a Loanee
Many private and public institutions offer student loans for post-educational purposes. Never lend your students or others money for their education unless you really don't expect them to pay you back. Many times lending money to people you know does not work and causes hard feelings. Public and private loans are for students' educational purposes and will cover things like courses, books, meal plans, and student housing cost. Most of these loans are lower interest and do not have any payments due until a period after the student graduates college. This allows for the student to attend school and focus on learning without having to worry about working too much and using their time trying to pay bills and not focusing on their schoolwork.

These are a good option if you must borrow money, but always try to work as much as possible to cover costs so that when you graduate college you have little debt. "Just Ask" yourself the value of your decisions. You may find that working too much while at college costs you more money if you are not able to get the needed grades to pursue the education required for the field in which you want to work. Remember that you will most likely make more money when you graduate and get a job in your field. Therefore, it may take a lot less work to pay off the loans you borrowed. For example, if you work ten hours a week at ten dollars an hour for a total of 100 per week and when you graduate you will be making twenty dollars an hour, you will end up working 50% less to pay off your debt. So, please, "Just Ask" yourself what is more valuable to you, working to end up with less debt in college or working less so you can get the needed education to make more money when you graduate?

Working for a Goal
If you are going to work, try to leverage your time and money to your advantage. For example, if you like to play golf and you get free golf by working at a golf course, then it may make sense to work there. That way you benefit by getting work experience, making money, and saving money. An internship in your field that pays you and offers you work experience may be a great option. I have known many people who got an internship from a company and were hired by them after they graduated school. If you get an internship, make sure you use it to your advantage and do your best to work hard and do a good job for the company. Many employers like people who ask for more things to do and volunteer to help others they work with when appropriate.

My whole career and leadership growth has come from what I call Servant Leadership. I think of Servant Leadership as an internal attitude that you are going to work with all members of the organization to support their needs and make them successful rather than worrying about your own internal selfish needs. I have always found if you help others first, you are always taken care of and grow in an organization. This means you can't be afraid to grow others into your boss or, at least, the type of boss you would like them to be. Think of it as you being a branch on a tree; if you help nurture and take care of the other branches, you will all grow together.

Scholarships
Scholarships come from many sources, so you should always be looking for opportunities. Scholarships can be provided based on many different criteria, such as merit, athletics, and fields of study, student nationality, college specific scholarships, gender, and more. It can be difficult to find some of these scholarships,

so you need to do a little research to find some that will work for you. You will be able to find some resources to help you at JustAskTheBook.com. Also, you should always go to career counselors, student aid departments at your university, other business in your field of study, and even your current employer to see if they are willing to offer you anything toward your education. You can search the internet for opportunities as well. Don't limit yourself to just a quick search. For example, if you want to work as an athletic director or teacher, you should call some people who are in that field and ask them for advice on how to best benefit from your education and if there are any scholarships or grants in your field that they could steer you toward.

Negotiating with Your Employer for More Money

Whether you are just out of school or working to get promoted in your current industry, you need to learn the basics of negotiation. A job interview is not the time to discuss finances or salary unless the employer specifically brings up the salary or benefits. Your number one goal should be to impress them with your talent and skills so you get the job you want and deserve. Once you have a job offer in hand, you can begin negotiations.

The first thing to look at is the salary. Many employers expect to bring an employee in at a salary that has a range of pay. Don't be afraid to ask for a little more money than what they are offering you. Also, don't be shy about asking for a set annual increase percentage or an annual salary increase based on performance. The key thing is to ask in a nice and non-confrontational way. Many times you can achieve up to 10% more than your initial offer by just asking up front if the salary is negotiable. If they say to you that they have a little flexibility, then they are prepared to work with you in the negotiation process. If they say that the offer is a "take it or leave it" offer, then you know you may not have any room to negotiate. However, if you don't ask for a little more money, the employer might think you are not a good negotiator, and I would hope you are not applying for a sales position. Part of the negotiations may be to thank the employer for the job offer and let them know that you are really looking forward to working with them and saving them money and bringing value to the organization. However, you were wondering if they may be able to increase the salary slightly.

Once you have the salary negotiations out of the way, you can ask for things like increases in moving allowances, maybe a curtain allowance (see "Just Ask for More Than You Need When Negotiating" in Chapter 8). I generally save the money for investments and don't use it unless it is really needed. If they offer a 401K savings plan with a set time before you are vested, you can "Just Ask" if they can make you fully vested coming onboard their company. Otherwise, a lot of companies may require three to five years of working to become fully vested in their 401K plan. If you leave the company before being fully vested, you may only get a percentage of their matching fund. If you were fully vested in your last company, there is no reason a new company should not match the same thing you had before being hired by them. Most companies do not expect you to take a loss to come work for them. However, they are not going to help you negotiate either.

Health insurance is one thing most companies will cover for you as well. So if your previous company's health insurance runs out before you qualify for insurance in your new job, ask the hiring company if they would be willing to cover your insurance so that you do not have a gap between employment. This has always been covered in my experience, so "Just Ask."

Negotiating the ability to work from home is becoming a more valuable and common part of job employment. Depending on your role, it may be a fair request to see if you could work from home one or two days a week. This not only saves you time and money in travel but also allows you the freedom to focus on your job in an environment that can make you more productive for the employer. When negotiating this type of request, emphasize to the employer that you are a responsible and dependable employee whose work will show results whether you work from home or at the office and that you would be available during the workday as needed.

Some other things you may be able to negotiate, depending on the role and the company, are: a cafeteria plan (free or reduced meal cost), a life insurance policy provided by the company, and vacation time. When you get to a new job, you should not expect to take a vacation hit. "Just Ask" the employer if they will match your previous vacation time. In fact, you should ask for more vacation than you had because you know you deserve it. Some companies are even offering unlimited vacation for employees. However, find out the precedence that has been set by high-performing employees so you can follow suit. I can guarantee you that if you take advantage of a system like this, your peers will hold you accountable and you may not have your job for long. I am sure there a few more things in job negotiating you can "Just Ask," so think about them, put a smile on your face, and don't be afraid to ask.

Funding Your Retirement Account

I have had a lot of people tell me they cannot afford to fund their retirement account. After speaking with them for a while, I learn they don't understand or know what it means to fund a retirement account. For example, if an employer is offering a matching 401K plan, then it is absolutely ridiculous not to at least fund their matching contribution. Again, you have to look at your goals and not just look at today. A 401K has many investment options, such as stocks, bonds, money market accounts, and more.

You can't allow not knowing how something works to prevent you from reaching your financial goals. You can go to a library and study more about 401K plans or speak with your company provider and "Just Ask" them to help you understand the plans and ask them for their advice based on your age and retirement goals. Maybe meet with several financial planners to understand your options. Also, understand that your 401K has many legal rights that your employer can't take away and that your money will always be yours. A 401K can be used for many things according to the laws by which they are managed. For example, at this time, some people can take out a home loan against their 401K to buy their first house. One drawback is that if you put money into a Traditional IRA or 401K and want to just take money out, you may be penalized an early withdrawal penalty along with taxes on the amount put into the account. Therefore, you have to be careful with how you manage the account. A 401K and other retirement plans can take up a whole book in itself. At a minimum, you need to understand the basics and meet with knowledgeable people to help you understand your options.

Many retirement accounts are a tax shelter, which means you don't pay taxes on the money until you withdraw it from the account when you retire. The thought behind this investment is that when you retire, the taxes you pay then will be less impactful than if you paid them today and did not invest the money. Therefore, if you make $50,000 a year and put $10,000 in your retirement account, you will only pay taxes that year on $40,000 instead of on the whole $50,000. Therefore, you will save the taxes that you would have paid on the additional $10,000 you invested. If your income tax rate is 18%, you would have saved $1,800 in taxes for that year. So it really only cost you about $8,200 in out-of-pocket expenses to invest the full $10,000 because you would have had to pay the $1,800 in taxes if you took it as income instead of putting it into your retirement. Please see my website at JustAskTheBook.com for more information.

Roth IRA

If you choose to invest the money after paying taxes, such as a Roth IRA, you can earn your money interest free, but you will have had to pay the taxes up front. If you earned $50,000 in income, you would have paid full taxes on the income and then invested the $10,000 into the account. The $10,000 cost you $1,800 in taxes. Therefore, when you withdraw the money at retirement, you will be able to take it out tax-free. The thought is for the money to grow to where you end up saving money at retirement age when you withdraw. One other advantage is that you can take your principle out from your Roth IRA account without tax penalty with today's tax laws. However, I recommend you see more information and resources on my website, JustAskTheBook.com.

"Just Ask" Yourself

- Ask yourself if working hard to get an education will pay off in the long run and if you are willing to put the extra effort in up front to benefit you long term.
- Ask yourself if you can be disciplined enough to put in for all available scholarships and grants by the due date.
- Ask yourself if your educational expenses will provide you with a job that you can enjoy doing for your lifetime or if you are only being educated for making money.
- Ask yourself if you can find a career and education that will provide you with the joy of helping others and still provide you the means to support yourself.
- Ask yourself if you really need a title or status type position to be happy.

"Just Ask" Others

- Ask college recruitment departments for additional grants or scholarships to help you attend their school.
- Ask for additional resources to help you attend the college of your choice, such as free books, used books, and discounted credit or housing costs.

- Ask for work studies, paid internships, or other duties that can help you pay for your education.
- Ask the companies in your field of study if they will help pay for your education if you work for them when you graduate.
- Ask other students and teachers in your field for advice on how to get work and pay for your education.
- Always negotiate with an employer for your benefits.
- Ask what type of retirement investment accounts are available at your place of employment. If you are self-employed, ask an accountant for direction on setting up a retirement account. Either way, you have to invest money to make money.

"Just Ask" Savings

"I asked the financial aid office at my college if they could help me cover the additional expenses above financial aid, and they provided me a work study that I loved and got paid for. I was an usher for hockey games, which I was paying to go to, and now I got in for free and got paid."

   —Chris H., Marquette, MI

"I asked a college professor if he had or knew of anyone with used books for sale. He actually had an old one he gave me for free and I saved $85."

   —Doug H., Grand Rapids, MI

"I asked my employer if they would help pay for my advanced education toward an MBA. They offered to pay $75,000 of the $100,000 fees if I committed to work for them for two years after receiving my degree and if I maintained a B average. I saved all this money and was able to advance my career with the company, and they paid for most of my education."

   —Pete A., Mequon, WI

"I asked some local companies who were in the field I wanted to work in if I could have an internship, and I saved over $50,000. They provided me an internship working for them, helped pay for my education, and offered me a job when I graduated."

   —Shelly L., Walla Walla, WA

"I asked a company that was hiring me for a new job if they would match my vacation, my 401K being 100% vested, and if they would provide me some moving costs. I made over $5,000."

   —Patrick S., Minong, WI

Chapter 11
How Long Will It Take to Become a Millionaire?

I was speaking to my sister one day and she shared with me that when she was younger she read a book about how much money a person could make by saving twenty dollars a week. When she and I spoke, she suggested sharing in my book how much money a person could make if they saved up a few dollars. I thought about her suggestion, and it was very clear that it would bring value to share with people how much money they could make by saving their money. I thought it would be helpful to show how much a person could earn by showing some savings calculations based on age. In fact, I took it a little further by showing actual numbers to give people incentive to follow a regimented savings plan.

Many people equate being a millionaire to being successful. However, I must warn you that "a million" is a symbolic number that represents a goal each person should set for themselves. For one person, $100,000 may be their millionaire goal and others may seek to be multimillionaires. No matter what your goals are, I want to personally encourage you to think beyond "How can I get more money for myself." I truly understand wanting to gain for yourself, but if you can mature in your internal understanding of the value of money, you will include others in your plans of becoming a millionaire. For example, you may have a favorite charity or organization that you can and will help by making more money. By having goals outside of yourself and working toward a monetary goal with others in mind, it will bring you more spiritual value and self-value than just striving for more money. Many times we are willing to work for the things that have value in our life, and most people want to help others.

Becoming a Millionaire Starts with Pennies

When I was a young child, my mother would always pick up pennies on the sidewalk and check for change inside the vending machines to see if someone left a few cents she could find. It was embarrassing for us as children when people saw her picking up pennies or sticking her fingers into the change slots on vending machines and pay telephones. We would always ask why she was doing that and she would respond, "Because pennies count." (For those of you who are younger, people had to put money into phones and phone booths to makes phones calls only a couple of decades ago.)

As I grew older and began to understand what she was doing and why, her picking up pennies gave me insight into the type of life she had as a child growing up during the Great Depression. I had to ask myself if being frugal with pennies was a good idea or not. What I saw her do for our family by saving a few pennies here and there was absolutely amazing. I really have come to appreciate her sacrifice and the value of a penny. Just practicing the principle of understanding that value of a penny will help a person focus on the details behind their expenses and hopefully allow them to ask themselves, before spending money or time, what impact it will have on them, the environment, and those around them. If one can keep track of the pennies, then keeping track of greater amounts will become easy, especially if you see money as a tool to benefit yourself and others.

Understanding the Value of Time
When I was thirteen, my father died unexpectedly and my mother ended up raising four teenage children on one income. We lived at what would be considered poverty level. However, my mother was able to budget and save without relying on the state for any support. During this time, she worked as a secretary for about $15,000 a year. She managed to save over a million pennies to keep us all in private school and provided us the best education possible. At that time, the education was probably somewhere around $2,000 a year or more per student. Sending four children to that school on a $15,000 a year salary did not leave much money for anything else. Some people may have thought of my mother as crazy for spending so much money on our grade school and high school education, but we appreciated it, and I truly feel that a good education benefited us all.

Families in the USA Have the Potential to Become Millionaires
Many families in the US have the opportunity to become millionaires but not in the sense that most of us think about. What do I mean by this? Well, for example, if a person works a job that pays $50,000 a year, and they work for twenty or more years at this rate, then you could say that they made over a million dollars in their life. However, we all know that even though a person may have earned over a million dollars, they would be lucky to have saved a small percentage of that.

So the real question is, how much do you have to save to be a millionaire and not how much do you have to make to be a millionaire. A person who makes $100,000 annually but only saves $10,000 a year is not as fortunate as the person who makes $60,000 a year and saves $25,000 a year. The person who saves more and invests the money wisely and brings the most gain is going to arrive at the millionaire finish line first. So, "Just Ask" yourself where you want to end up as you consider all the purchases we have discussed in this book.

Spending on Your Education Can Save You Money
According to the National Association of Colleges and Employees (NACE) 2018 Summer Survey, the average new graduate starting salary currently stands at $50,516. If you make $50,000 a year, which is the average salary of a college student who graduated in 2017, and you save 25% of your money and invest it into a 6% investment with monthly payment of $1,041, it would only take you thirty years to become a millionaire. On the next few pages, I will share some numbers that were calculated to show how the amount and time you save can affect your future potential savings.

Don't Spend like the Boxers
Let's figure out how you can become a millionaire because it can be very motivational if you can set a goal that will drive you to success. If you make $100,000 a year or more, you may never become a millionaire. In fact, many people we think of as millionaires often don't end up keeping all their money. This is because many of them do not know the value of the money they have and are too busy spending it as if the source of their income will never run out. For example, let's say that you are a world-class boxer who made millions in your career like Mike Tyson. If you spend a lot of your money on a large house, fancy cars, and lavish things during your career, you may not have enough after the fighting days are over to keep that lifestyle. Today it is Floyd Mayweather and Connor McGregor who could be next if they are not careful.

It is important to always think ahead about what you will have at the end of your career, instead of just spending today because you have the money. You have to think about what will happen if you lose your income source or if life changes. What example do you want to leave behind to others and your family?

I look at Warren Buffet as a prime example of a person who has lived a fairly frugal lifestyle, even though he is one of the richest people in the world. I have read several news articles that state he is not going to leave his wealth to his family but plans to use it to help others. I think he truly knows he cannot take his wealth with him and that it is just a tool for helping others.

Only 3–4% of Americans are lucky enough to be worth a million dollars. So, set your expectations up correctly in your mind. It is good to have goals, but don't be disappointed if you don't get there. And even if you do get there, you could still be struggling financially and feel broke. I know that may not be what you want to hear, but it is reality. Being classified as a millionaire is just a number that is given to people based on their net worth. Therefore, you could own a $500,000 home, $55,000 in furniture, two cars valued at $50,000 each, a $300,000 vacation home, and have $50,000 in the bank and be considered a millionaire. However, you may be broke trying to pay all the taxes, insurance, maintenance, and so on trying to keep your millionaire status. Therefore, be careful and think ahead about what it takes to be a millionaire and what it will take to keep all that you have worked so hard for.

Some people don't have the discipline and will not save their money because they feel they need to have a large house, a big boat, and a lot of other things to bring them internal worth and happiness. Also, some of the wealthiest people I have known are unhappy because they keep striving for material things that won't bring them true happiness internally. At some point they find their needs and wants can't be satisfied. That's why I continue to caution you that part of your goals must be to have goals to invest in things that bring you eternal happiness. Many times your religious foundation and a desire to help others around you can keep you grounded and bring you an internal sense of fulfillment and joy.

Decreasing Your Wants Today Will Increase Your Net Worth Tomorrow

Unless you are extremely focused, it will take forever to become a millionaire if you keep a mentality of always wanting bigger and more expensive things. It is likely that you have a greater risk or going broke than if you stayed poor and had to struggle for every penny. Even if you are fortunate enough to win the lottery or have someone leave you a lot of money in their will, you need to plan to work and save. Getting a large inheritance or winning the lottery may be unlikely to occur and will lead to more trouble because you have not learned the principles of earning and saving your own money. Therefore, if you learn anything from this book, you need to ask your internal self if you can handle the winnings. If you can't handle them, you must find someone trustworthy to help you manage yourself with your best interests in mind. Your goal should be to preserve principle at this point and not to put money into risky investments to try to make more of something you don't need more of.

Also, you have to find something to do that fulfills your passions and keeps you busy working on things you love. Your hobbies will soon become boring if that is all you do; they will become work too, and you will end up hating your life. Get grounded ASAP if you hit the big windfall. The best way to do this is by helping others. Serve at a local food bank, help out at a charity, volunteer at your church, set up a community garden on your land, mentor children, or go on a mission trip to help others. No matter what you do, ground yourself and surround yourself with other people who will spiritually help raise you up to a higher level and not have their own selfish interests in mind.

Be careful not to surround yourself with new people who have an interest in stealing and spending your money for you. If you do this, you will soon find yourself worse off than before you acquired recent wealth. Of course, you will have the best friends money can buy, at least until the money runs out, and then most of them disappear. You will need moral, ethical people to help you. I would recommend working with at least two different people who are from different areas of expertise so that they can help keep each other in line and not get tempted to take advantage of you. That is why you should only confide in trusted sources. Tons of people will tell you any story or make you feel guilty in order to get your money. If you give some of your wealth away, assure it is to a good cause and that you are not being taken advantage of.

Have a good accountant and other leaders you can trust with your financial information. Set up a will in case something bad happens to you. Do this while you are young, just in case. You can always modify this later in life if your family or goals change, but not having one leaves people fighting over assets they did not have to work hard to get. Also, many families split up over monetary assets left behind.

Most people who win the lottery or get money given to them without learning how to manage their finances end up losing more than they started with. However, if you train yourself to follow some of the principles in my book, you are more likely to succeed in managing any good fortune you may come across and sharing your gains with others. Keep in mind that it is not how much you make but how much you save that will drive you to be financially successful.

Develop a Budget and Savings Goals

Most successful people who make extra money have financial savings and budget goals. You must have a budget that allows you to look at your incoming money and what you are spending it on. Your budget can be as simple as a sheet of paper with your weekly income versus your weekly expenses, or you can get more elaborate by having a computer program for budgeting. It really does not matter what type of budget you have, but it is important to know what you have coming in as income and what you have going out for expenses.

A simple budget would show the amount of money you get each week, actual expenses, and remaining money for other non-expense items. When you make your budget, be sure to include things you must be able to pay, such as electric bills, gas bills, auto payments, house payments, taxes, insurance, and groceries.

Analyze What You Are Spending Money On

If you find that the amount of money coming in cannot cover your expenses, you have to make a lifestyle change to make sure you can make ends meet. If on paper you have extra money, but each month you find that you are behind, a budget will show you where your money is going, and you can choose to make changes to benefit you. For example, if you make $2,000 a month and you find that your bills are only $1,500 per month, you should have $500 left a month for non-expenses. However, if you end up putting $500 on your credit card each month instead of having $500 extra in cash, you need to find what you are over-spending on. You may find it is as simple as going out to eat too much. No matter what you find, it is important to find it so that you can be the one to choose what you spend your money on. You are the boss of your own financial destiny and can decide if you want to cut back today so you can spend more tomorrow.

Play with Saving Scenarios so You Can See Your Goals

For example, if I make $18,000 a year and save 25% of my income or $375 a month and invest it at 6% interest, it would only take forty-seven years to be a millionaire. If you make $50,000 a year and only invest 10% of your income, which is about $416 a month, it would only take you forty-three years to save a million dollars. Most people cannot look that far into the future, so sometimes is it easier to look at the number on a spreadsheet or graph. That is why you should go to my website, JustAskTheBook.com, to use my millionaire calculator so that you can see an actual savings timeline to hit your goals. Also, I have added a giving calculator so you can put in a certain percentage of your income for giving as well to help you stay focused as you grow to your millionaire status.

Set up Automatic Deduction into Your Online Savings Account

If you find it is too difficult for you to take the extra money each month and save it, set up an automatic bank withdrawal from your paycheck to a savings account. It is better to start small, and as you watch it grow, it will give you more incentive to put more in. I remember how long it took to save my first $100, and then it seemed to take forever to save $1,000, and then $10,000, and so on. However, as I got closer to each goal, I noticed I was always more diligent in my savings to help me beat the next hurdle. There were times when I remember having so much momentum and wanting to make a larger payment to get there more quickly so I could celebrate. One easy tool I have set up is an online link to several places where you can set up a savings account, which you can do just by visiting JustAskTheBook.com.

Celebrate the Little Successes

So many times we reach a goal and we forget to celebrate our successes. By celebrating your success, you reinforce in your brain that what you are doing is a good thing, and it will help make it easier to continue reaching your goals. For example, if I hit my $100 savings goal, I am going to treat myself to ice cream. If I pay my mortgage off early, I am going to buy the new bike I have always wanted. No matter what the goal is, have some type of reward. Just be careful not to over-reward yourself and get back in debt.

Breaking the Chains of Debt

Once you break the chains and become debt free, it is so much easier to manage your money because you will not want to be in the position of owing anyone for anything. Therefore, if you can meet a goal of being debt free on everything, including your house, then you will be able to do so much more to help yourself and others. Just keep focused and have your goals in mind and do not let others frustrate you or take your focus from the goals. Always continue to surround yourself with positive and caring people who support your goals, and you will achieve more than you ever thought you could financially and spiritually. Good luck and keep on living out your dreams.

Use Free Online Tools

I would recommend going to JustAskTheBook.com and using several of the free bank calculation tools to determine your numbers to becoming a millionaire based on your salary and savings goals. Or you can even go to a local bank or investment firm and "Just Ask" them to help you calculate how much you have to save to hit your financial goals.

Below are a few generic charts I made using a free Excel spreadsheet template called "Retirement Calculator," which was provided when I did a search of my Microsoft Office tools. I created some examples using the ages twenty, thirty, and forty. However, you can enter any age when you visit my website. The following charts and graphs show how long it would take to become a millionaire if you made $50,000 a year and invested 25% of your income in an account with a 6% return on your investment. I wanted to keep this basic, so I did not show any increases in salary over the years or any inflation or cost of living allowances. I did not show any higher rate of return than the 6% because I wanted my numbers to be realistic to the swings in the market that may occur. Also, I have included a calculation of how much money you would make if you saved twenty dollars a week, as my sister suggested. Take a look at the charts at the end of this chapter to see what you need to save to become a millionaire.

"Just Ask" Yourself

- Ask yourself if you are willing to work hard today and sacrifice so you can be a millionaire tomorrow.
- Ask yourself what it means to your internal being to become a millionaire.

- Ask yourself what type of example you want to be to others and how your examples can reflect your values.
- Ask yourself how long it will take you to hit your financial goals and what you are willing to sacrifice to reach them.
- Ask yourself if becoming a millionaire will help you help others and be more generous with your assets or if it will cause you to want more and cling to your wealth even tighter.

"Just Ask" Others

- Ask for help from JustAskTheBook.com.
- Ask for help from others you know who are successful.
- Ask professional accountants and financial advisors how some of the retirement investments work if you don't understand them.
- Ask your company's financial people and their investment companies for help in understanding the right retirement plan for you.
- Ask other like-minded people you trust for guidance and to brainstorm options for your investments so you can hit your goals.
- Ask a charitable organization if you can volunteer to help others.

"Just Ask" Savings

"I asked the financial advisor to help me lay out a savings plan to help me meet my financial goals. They met with me for free and helped me invest my savings to be able to make over $1,000,000 in twenty-three years, and I retired early and spend my time volunteering at the church and helping others."

   —Dick S., Madison, WI

"I asked my good friend to help me build an Excel spreadsheet to track my expenses, and they helped me for free. I have now saved over $10,000 my first year by just watching what I spend my money on."

   —Michael H., Keen, NH

"I asked a cousin of mine for a good book editor when writing a book to help people. The book editor she provided helped me finalize my book, and I was able to help people with a lot of the techniques mentioned. I met my life dream of publishing a book by just asking."

   —Chris H., Stevens Point, WI

"I asked the local bank to help me set up a savings account, and they gave me $300 for free just for signing up for the account and putting in an initial deposit."

—Laura C., Connell, WA

"I asked myself what I wanted to do for a living and how much money I needed to be happy. I was able to lay out my goals and meet my financial goals to retire. I now travel the world as a missionary helping others."

—Pastor John H., Hatti, Africa

At age twenty, you can save enough to retire at fifty-eight with over $1.6 million dollars.

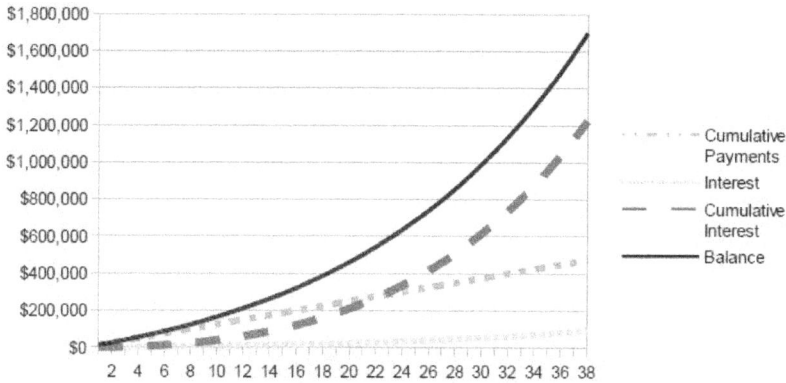

Year	Age	Rate	Invested (Payment)	Cumulative Payments	Interest	Cumulative Interest	Balance
0			$0.00	$0.00	$0.00	$0.00	$0.00
1	21	6.00%	$12,500.00	$12,500.00	$0.00	$0.00	$12,500.00
2	22	6.00%	$12,500.00	$25,000.00	$750.00	$750.00	$25,750.00
3	23	6.00%	$12,500.00	$37,500.00	$1,545.00	$2,295.00	$39,795.00
4	24	6.00%	$12,500.00	$50,000.00	$2,387.70	$4,682.70	$54,682.70
5	25	6.00%	$12,500.00	$62,500.00	$3,280.96	$7,963.66	$70,463.66
6	26	6.00%	$12,500.00	$75,000.00	$4,227.82	$12,191.48	$87,191.48
7	27	6.00%	$12,500.00	$87,500.00	$5,231.49	$17,422.97	$104,922.97
8	28	6.00%	$12,500.00	$100,000.00	$6,295.38	$23,718.35	$123,718.35
9	29	6.00%	$12,500.00	$112,500.00	$7,423.10	$31,141.45	$143,641.45
10	30	6.00%	$12,500.00	$125,000.00	$8,618.49	$39,759.94	$164,759.94
11	31	6.00%	$12,500.00	$137,500.00	$9,885.60	$49,645.53	$187,145.53
12	32	6.00%	$12,500.00	$150,000.00	$11,228.73	$60,874.26	$210,874.26
13	33	6.00%	$12,500.00	$162,500.00	$12,652.46	$73,526.72	$236,026.72
14	34	6.00%	$12,500.00	$175,000.00	$14,161.60	$87,688.32	$262,688.32
15	35	6.00%	$12,500.00	$187,500.00	$15,761.30	$103,449.62	$290,949.62
16	36	6.00%	$12,500.00	$200,000.00	$17,456.98	$120,906.60	$320,906.60
17	37	6.00%	$12,500.00	$212,500.00	$19,254.40	$140,161.00	$352,661.00
18	38	6.00%	$12,500.00	$225,000.00	$21,159.66	$161,320.66	$386,320.66
19	39	6.00%	$12,500.00	$237,500.00	$23,179.24	$184,499.90	$421,999.90
20	40	6.00%	$12,500.00	$250,000.00	$25,319.99	$209,819.89	$459,819.89
21	41	6.00%	$12,500.00	$262,500.00	$27,589.19	$237,409.08	$499,909.08
22	42	6.00%	$12,500.00	$275,000.00	$29,994.55	$267,403.63	$542,403.63
23	43	6.00%	$12,500.00	$287,500.00	$32,544.22	$299,947.85	$587,447.85
24	44	6.00%	$12,500.00	$300,000.00	$35,246.87	$335,194.72	$635,194.72
25	45	6.00%	$12,500.00	$312,500.00	$38,111.68	$373,306.40	$685,806.40
26	46	6.00%	$12,500.00	$325,000.00	$41,148.38	$414,454.78	$739,454.78
27	47	6.00%	$12,500.00	$337,500.00	$44,367.29	$458,822.07	$796,322.07
28	48	6.00%	$12,500.00	$350,000.00	$47,779.32	$506,601.40	$856,601.40
29	49	6.00%	$12,500.00	$362,500.00	$51,396.08	$557,997.48	$920,497.48
30	50	6.00%	$12,500.00	$375,000.00	$55,229.85	$613,227.33	$988,227.33
31	51	6.00%	$12,500.00	$387,500.00	$59,293.64	$672,520.97	$1,060,020.97
32	52	6.00%	$12,500.00	$400,000.00	$63,601.26	$736,122.23	$1,136,122.23
33	53	6.00%	$12,500.00	$412,500.00	$68,167.33	$804,289.56	$1,216,789.56
34	54	6.00%	$12,500.00	$425,000.00	$73,007.37	$877,296.93	$1,302,296.93
35	55	6.00%	$12,500.00	$437,500.00	$78,137.82	$955,434.75	$1,392,934.75
36	56	6.00%	$12,500.00	$450,000.00	$83,576.08	$1,039,010.83	$1,489,010.83
37	57	6.00%	$12,500.00	$462,500.00	$89,340.65	$1,128,351.48	$1,590,851.48
38	58	6.00%	$12,500.00	$475,000.00	$95,451.09	$1,223,802.57	$1,698,802.57

At age twenty, if you save $1,040 a year ($20/week), you will earn over $140,000 by age fifty-eight.

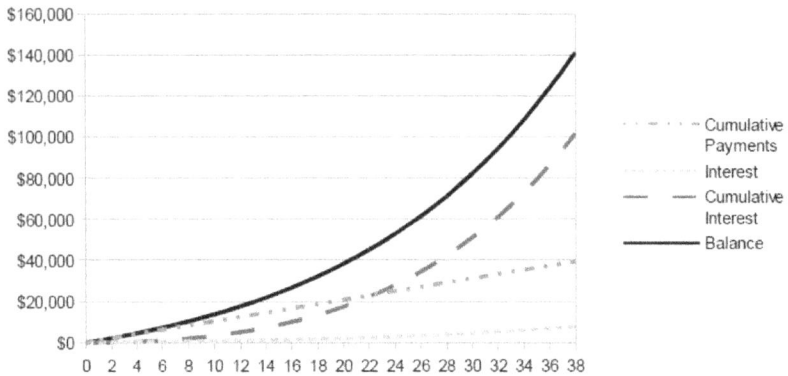

Year	Age	Rate	Invested (Payment)	Cumulative Payments	Interest	Cumulative Interest	Balance
0			$0.00	$0.00	$0.00	$0.00	$0.00
1	21	6.00%	$1,040.00	$1,040.00	$0.00	$0.00	$1,040.00
2	22	6.00%	$1,040.00	$2,080.00	$62.40	$62.40	$2,142.40
3	23	6.00%	$1,040.00	$3,120.00	$128.54	$190.94	$3,310.94
4	24	6.00%	$1,040.00	$4,160.00	$198.66	$389.60	$4,549.60
5	25	6.00%	$1,040.00	$5,200.00	$272.98	$662.58	$5,862.58
6	26	6.00%	$1,040.00	$6,240.00	$351.75	$1,014.33	$7,254.33
7	27	6.00%	$1,040.00	$7,280.00	$435.26	$1,449.59	$8,729.59
8	28	6.00%	$1,040.00	$8,320.00	$523.78	$1,973.37	$10,293.37
9	29	6.00%	$1,040.00	$9,360.00	$617.60	$2,590.97	$11,950.97
10	30	6.00%	$1,040.00	$10,400.00	$717.06	$3,308.03	$13,708.03
11	31	6.00%	$1,040.00	$11,440.00	$822.48	$4,130.51	$15,570.51
12	32	6.00%	$1,040.00	$12,480.00	$934.23	$5,064.74	$17,544.74
13	33	6.00%	$1,040.00	$13,520.00	$1,052.68	$6,117.42	$19,637.42
14	34	6.00%	$1,040.00	$14,560.00	$1,178.25	$7,295.67	$21,855.67
15	35	6.00%	$1,040.00	$15,600.00	$1,311.34	$8,607.01	$24,207.01
16	36	6.00%	$1,040.00	$16,640.00	$1,452.42	$10,059.43	$26,699.43
17	37	6.00%	$1,040.00	$17,680.00	$1,601.97	$11,661.39	$29,341.39
18	38	6.00%	$1,040.00	$18,720.00	$1,760.48	$13,421.88	$32,141.88
19	39	6.00%	$1,040.00	$19,760.00	$1,928.51	$15,350.39	$35,110.39
20	40	6.00%	$1,040.00	$20,800.00	$2,106.62	$17,457.01	$38,257.01
21	41	6.00%	$1,040.00	$21,840.00	$2,295.42	$19,752.44	$41,592.44
22	42	6.00%	$1,040.00	$22,880.00	$2,495.55	$22,247.98	$45,127.98
23	43	6.00%	$1,040.00	$23,920.00	$2,707.68	$24,955.66	$48,875.66
24	44	6.00%	$1,040.00	$24,960.00	$2,932.54	$27,888.20	$52,848.20
25	45	6.00%	$1,040.00	$26,000.00	$3,170.89	$31,059.09	$57,059.09
26	46	6.00%	$1,040.00	$27,040.00	$3,423.55	$34,482.64	$61,522.64
27	47	6.00%	$1,040.00	$28,080.00	$3,691.36	$38,174.00	$66,254.00
28	48	6.00%	$1,040.00	$29,120.00	$3,975.24	$42,149.24	$71,269.24
29	49	6.00%	$1,040.00	$30,160.00	$4,276.15	$46,425.39	$76,585.39
30	50	6.00%	$1,040.00	$31,200.00	$4,595.12	$51,020.51	$82,220.51
31	51	6.00%	$1,040.00	$32,240.00	$4,933.23	$55,953.74	$88,193.74
32	52	6.00%	$1,040.00	$33,280.00	$5,291.62	$61,245.37	$94,525.37
33	53	6.00%	$1,040.00	$34,320.00	$5,671.52	$66,916.89	$101,236.89
34	54	6.00%	$1,040.00	$35,360.00	$6,074.21	$72,991.10	$108,351.10
35	55	6.00%	$1,040.00	$36,400.00	$6,501.07	$79,492.17	$115,892.17
36	56	6.00%	$1,040.00	$37,440.00	$6,953.53	$86,445.70	$123,885.70
37	57	6.00%	$1,040.00	$38,480.00	$7,433.14	$93,878.84	$132,358.84
38	58	6.00%	$1,040.00	$39,520.00	$7,941.53	$101,820.37	$141,340.37

At age thirty you can save enough to retire at sixty-one with over a million dollars.

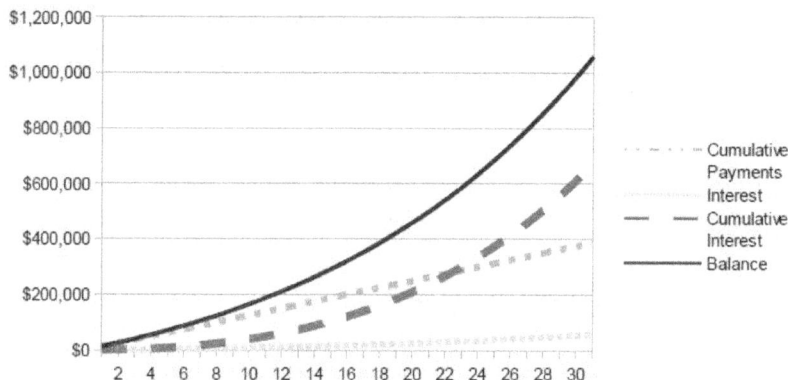

Year	Age	Rate	Invested (Payment)	Cumulative Payments	Interest	Cumulative Interest	Balance
0			$0.00	$0.00	$0.00	$0.00	$0.00
1	31	6.00%	$12,500.00	$12,500.00	$0.00	$0.00	$12,500.00
2	32	6.00%	$12,500.00	$25,000.00	$750.00	$750.00	$25,750.00
3	33	6.00%	$12,500.00	$37,500.00	$1,545.00	$2,295.00	$39,795.00
4	34	6.00%	$12,500.00	$50,000.00	$2,387.70	$4,682.70	$54,682.70
5	35	6.00%	$12,500.00	$62,500.00	$3,280.96	$7,963.66	$70,463.66
6	36	6.00%	$12,500.00	$75,000.00	$4,227.82	$12,191.48	$87,191.48
7	37	6.00%	$12,500.00	$87,500.00	$5,231.49	$17,422.97	$104,922.97
8	38	6.00%	$12,500.00	$100,000.00	$6,295.38	$23,718.35	$123,718.35
9	39	6.00%	$12,500.00	$112,500.00	$7,423.10	$31,141.45	$143,641.45
10	40	6.00%	$12,500.00	$125,000.00	$8,618.49	$39,759.94	$164,759.94
11	41	6.00%	$12,500.00	$137,500.00	$9,885.60	$49,645.53	$187,145.53
12	42	6.00%	$12,500.00	$150,000.00	$11,228.73	$60,874.26	$210,874.26
13	43	6.00%	$12,500.00	$162,500.00	$12,652.46	$73,526.72	$236,026.72
14	44	6.00%	$12,500.00	$175,000.00	$14,161.60	$87,688.32	$262,688.32
15	45	6.00%	$12,500.00	$187,500.00	$15,761.30	$103,449.62	$290,949.62
16	46	6.00%	$12,500.00	$200,000.00	$17,456.98	$120,906.60	$320,906.60
17	47	6.00%	$12,500.00	$212,500.00	$19,254.40	$140,161.00	$352,661.00
18	48	6.00%	$12,500.00	$225,000.00	$21,159.66	$161,320.66	$386,320.66
19	49	6.00%	$12,500.00	$237,500.00	$23,179.24	$184,499.90	$421,999.90
20	50	6.00%	$12,500.00	$250,000.00	$25,319.99	$209,819.89	$459,819.89
21	51	6.00%	$12,500.00	$262,500.00	$27,589.19	$237,409.08	$499,909.08
22	52	6.00%	$12,500.00	$275,000.00	$29,994.55	$267,403.63	$542,403.63
23	53	6.00%	$12,500.00	$287,500.00	$32,544.22	$299,947.85	$587,447.85
24	54	6.00%	$12,500.00	$300,000.00	$35,246.87	$335,194.72	$635,194.72
25	55	6.00%	$12,500.00	$312,500.00	$38,111.68	$373,306.40	$685,806.40
26	56	6.00%	$12,500.00	$325,000.00	$41,148.38	$414,454.78	$739,454.78
27	57	6.00%	$12,500.00	$337,500.00	$44,367.29	$458,822.07	$796,322.07
28	58	6.00%	$12,500.00	$350,000.00	$47,779.32	$506,601.40	$856,601.40
29	59	6.00%	$12,500.00	$362,500.00	$51,396.08	$557,997.48	$920,497.48
30	60	6.00%	$12,500.00	$375,000.00	$55,229.85	$613,227.33	$988,227.33
31	61	6.00%	$12,500.00	$387,500.00	$59,293.64	$672,520.97	$1,060,020.97

At age thirty, you can save $1,040 a year ($20/month) and retire at sixty-one with over $88,000 if you invest at 6%.

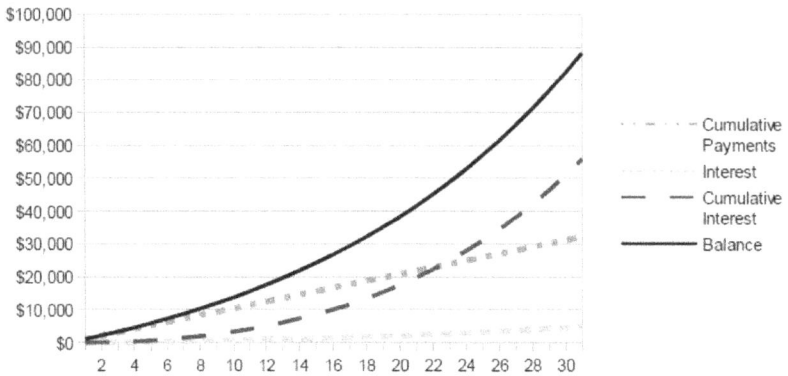

Year	Age	Rate	Invested (Payment)	Cumulative Payments	Interest	Cumulative Interest	Balance
0			$0.00	$0.00	$0.00	$0.00	$0.00
1	31	6.00%	$1,040.00	$1,040.00	$0.00	$0.00	$1,040.00
2	32	6.00%	$1,040.00	$2,080.00	$62.40	$62.40	$2,142.40
3	33	6.00%	$1,040.00	$3,120.00	$128.54	$190.94	$3,310.94
4	34	6.00%	$1,040.00	$4,160.00	$198.66	$389.60	$4,549.60
5	35	6.00%	$1,040.00	$5,200.00	$272.98	$662.58	$5,862.58
6	36	6.00%	$1,040.00	$6,240.00	$351.75	$1,014.33	$7,254.33
7	37	6.00%	$1,040.00	$7,280.00	$435.26	$1,449.59	$8,729.59
8	38	6.00%	$1,040.00	$8,320.00	$523.78	$1,973.37	$10,293.37
9	39	6.00%	$1,040.00	$9,360.00	$617.60	$2,590.97	$11,950.97
10	40	6.00%	$1,040.00	$10,400.00	$717.06	$3,308.03	$13,708.03
11	41	6.00%	$1,040.00	$11,440.00	$822.48	$4,130.51	$15,570.51
12	42	6.00%	$1,040.00	$12,480.00	$934.23	$5,064.74	$17,544.74
13	43	6.00%	$1,040.00	$13,520.00	$1,052.68	$6,117.42	$19,637.42
14	44	6.00%	$1,040.00	$14,560.00	$1,178.25	$7,295.67	$21,855.67
15	45	6.00%	$1,040.00	$15,600.00	$1,311.34	$8,607.01	$24,207.01
16	46	6.00%	$1,040.00	$16,640.00	$1,452.42	$10,059.43	$26,699.43
17	47	6.00%	$1,040.00	$17,680.00	$1,601.97	$11,661.39	$29,341.39
18	48	6.00%	$1,040.00	$18,720.00	$1,760.48	$13,421.88	$32,141.88
19	49	6.00%	$1,040.00	$19,760.00	$1,928.51	$15,350.39	$35,110.39
20	50	6.00%	$1,040.00	$20,800.00	$2,106.62	$17,457.01	$38,257.01
21	51	6.00%	$1,040.00	$21,840.00	$2,295.42	$19,752.44	$41,592.44
22	52	6.00%	$1,040.00	$22,880.00	$2,495.55	$22,247.98	$45,127.98
23	53	6.00%	$1,040.00	$23,920.00	$2,707.68	$24,955.66	$48,875.66
24	54	6.00%	$1,040.00	$24,960.00	$2,932.54	$27,888.20	$52,848.20
25	55	6.00%	$1,040.00	$26,000.00	$3,170.89	$31,059.09	$57,059.09
26	56	6.00%	$1,040.00	$27,040.00	$3,423.55	$34,482.64	$61,522.64
27	57	6.00%	$1,040.00	$28,080.00	$3,691.36	$38,174.00	$66,254.00
28	58	6.00%	$1,040.00	$29,120.00	$3,975.24	$42,149.24	$71,269.24
29	59	6.00%	$1,040.00	$30,160.00	$4,276.15	$46,425.39	$76,585.39
30	60	6.00%	$1,040.00	$31,200.00	$4,595.12	$51,020.51	$82,220.51
31	61	6.00%	$1,040.00	$32,240.00	$4,933.23	$55,953.74	$88,193.74

At age forty, you can save enough to retire at seventy-one with over a million dollars if you make $50,000 and invest 25% of your earnings at 6% interest.

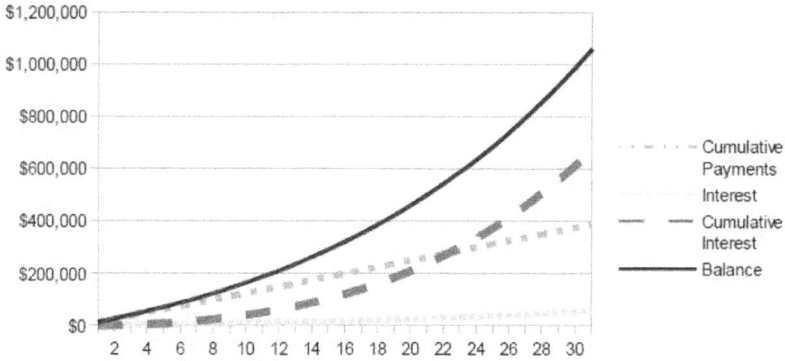

Year	Age	Rate	Invested (Payment)	Cumulative Payments	Interest	Cumulative Interest	Balance
0			$0.00	$0.00	$0.00	$0.00	$0.00
1	41	6.00%	$12,500.00	$12,500.00	$0.00	$0.00	$12,500.00
2	42	6.00%	$12,500.00	$25,000.00	$750.00	$750.00	$25,750.00
3	43	6.00%	$12,500.00	$37,500.00	$1,545.00	$2,295.00	$39,795.00
4	44	6.00%	$12,500.00	$50,000.00	$2,387.70	$4,682.70	$54,682.70
5	45	6.00%	$12,500.00	$62,500.00	$3,280.96	$7,963.66	$70,463.66
6	46	6.00%	$12,500.00	$75,000.00	$4,227.82	$12,191.48	$87,191.48
7	47	6.00%	$12,500.00	$87,500.00	$5,231.49	$17,422.97	$104,922.97
8	48	6.00%	$12,500.00	$100,000.00	$6,295.38	$23,718.35	$123,718.35
9	49	6.00%	$12,500.00	$112,500.00	$7,423.10	$31,141.45	$143,641.45
10	50	6.00%	$12,500.00	$125,000.00	$8,618.49	$39,759.94	$164,759.94
11	51	6.00%	$12,500.00	$137,500.00	$9,885.60	$49,645.53	$187,145.53
12	52	6.00%	$12,500.00	$150,000.00	$11,228.73	$60,874.26	$210,874.26
13	53	6.00%	$12,500.00	$162,500.00	$12,652.46	$73,526.72	$236,026.72
14	54	6.00%	$12,500.00	$175,000.00	$14,161.60	$87,688.32	$262,688.32
15	55	6.00%	$12,500.00	$187,500.00	$15,761.30	$103,449.62	$290,949.62
16	56	6.00%	$12,500.00	$200,000.00	$17,456.98	$120,906.60	$320,906.60
17	57	6.00%	$12,500.00	$212,500.00	$19,254.40	$140,161.00	$352,661.00
18	58	6.00%	$12,500.00	$225,000.00	$21,159.66	$161,320.66	$386,320.66
19	59	6.00%	$12,500.00	$237,500.00	$23,179.24	$184,499.90	$421,999.90
20	60	6.00%	$12,500.00	$250,000.00	$25,319.99	$209,819.89	$459,819.89
21	61	6.00%	$12,500.00	$262,500.00	$27,589.19	$237,409.08	$499,909.08
22	62	6.00%	$12,500.00	$275,000.00	$29,994.55	$267,403.63	$542,403.63
23	63	6.00%	$12,500.00	$287,500.00	$32,544.22	$299,947.85	$587,447.85
24	64	6.00%	$12,500.00	$300,000.00	$35,246.87	$335,194.72	$635,194.72
25	65	6.00%	$12,500.00	$312,500.00	$38,111.68	$373,306.40	$685,806.40
26	66	6.00%	$12,500.00	$325,000.00	$41,148.38	$414,454.78	$739,454.78
27	67	6.00%	$12,500.00	$337,500.00	$44,367.29	$458,822.07	$796,322.07
28	68	6.00%	$12,500.00	$350,000.00	$47,779.32	$506,601.40	$856,601.40
29	69	6.00%	$12,500.00	$362,500.00	$51,396.08	$557,997.48	$920,497.48
30	70	6.00%	$12,500.00	$375,000.00	$55,229.85	$613,227.33	$988,227.33
31	71	6.00%	$12,500.00	$387,500.00	$59,293.64	$672,520.97	$1,060,020.97

Acknowledgments

I debated whether I wanted to include anything in my book about my spiritual beliefs, but I think it is important people understand that Jesus Christ is my Lord and Savior and the One who has empowered me to be all I can be. The Bible, which I believe is the Holy Word of God, gives us guidance in our daily life. God's Word has inspired me and has led me to see the importance of managing my finances and helping others.

I decided to include personal stories in my "Thank You" and "Preface" section as well as throughout my book as I believe it will help you, the reader, understand where I am coming from. It will become clear to you how and why I learned to handle money as you read on.

There are many people I thank for making it possible for me to write this book and giving me inspiration along the way. I want to thank my mother, Lillian, who was creative and inspired my creativity; my brother, John, who is always sharing business strategies; my sister Heidi, who inspires me with her compassion and caring; and my sister Margaret, who has been encouraging me to complete my book and has amazing creativity.

Next, I want to thank my wonderful, loving wife, who took the time to proofread my book and give me great feedback, and my son and daughter for always asking me to read them the stories in my book. My children were not afraid to laugh at some of my stories and ask me, "Dad, did that really happen?" I also want to thank my in-laws who are a living example of generosity. They are always giving and helping others and expect nothing in return. They are there for us and share much love with our family. It is great to be loved and to love!

In addition to family, the following people mentioned were also instrumental in my life and some of their stories are mentioned in my book.

I thank my Michigan neighbors-like-family for taking me to church when I was a teenager. They were influential spiritual leaders and provided me guidance. They not only nurtured me when I was hungry by feeding me but also taught me about the importance of tithing and giving to promote the Lord's work. I grew up as close to them as I did my biological family and appreciate all they have done for me.

I want to thank one of my friends, Dave, who helped me learn a lot about finance and investing. Dave has always been a great teacher and has patience unlike anyone I have ever known. He helped me become smarter with my finances and understand the stock market. He retired at forty-five years of age and is still retired and is in his sixties as I write this book, so he must know something.

In addition, I thank my Washington State friends, Gerry and Kathy, who helped us so much when we moved to Washington just after our college years. (My wife was completing her master's degree, and I was completing my Bachelor of Science degree.) They became like our parents away from home. Without Gerry's encouragement, I might never have completed my college degree. They truly were and still are some of our best friends.

I want to thank our other friends in Washington, Terry and Laura, who are wonderful friends with whom we have enjoyed so many wonderful adventures over the past twenty-three years. Laura passed away after a seven-year battle with bone cancer, but she is in our hearts always and in my book from all that she gave to help others.

Additionally, I thank Ann and Clay, who always gave us good sound financial and employment advice when we moved to Illinois. They became some of our best friends as well.

Another person I owe a big thank you too is Richard Nixon, who encouraged me to finish my book after so many years and gave me a copy of his book, *Tenant in a House of Clay*, along with other financial books for review and inspiration. One of the most important things he taught me was to surround myself with people who are a positive influence and support my goals and vision.

I want to thank my editor, Rosemi Mederos, who did a fantastic job of helping me bring my vision to life along with providing me personal encouragement to achieve my dream of publishing a book to help others. Just as she has helped so many, I hope my book does the same for you.

I am thankful to be friends with: Don, Kay, and Owen; Philip Sr., Phil Jr., and Dee; Richard, Frank, Pete, and Julie; and the class of 1989 from Notre Dame High School, Harper Woods, Michigan. (Go Irish.)

About the Author

Chris Hetherman is a Certified Financial Representative and the author of various technical articles focused on helping people. He's a dedicated husband and father of two children along with a caretaker of sixteen chickens, three goats, two dogs, a cat, and a rabbit on his small hobby farm in Central Wisconsin. He wrote *Just Ask* as a survival guide for today's economy based on real-life experiences from which anyone can benefit.

JustAsktheBook.com

www.ingramcontent.com/pod-product-compliance
Lightning Source LLC
Chambersburg PA
CBHW020838210326
41598CB00019B/1947